NUTSHELLS

EU Law

FIRST EDITION

Round Hall's Nutshell, Nutcase, Exam Focus, and Legal Skills Series

NUTSHELL TITLES

Specially written for students of Irish law, each title in the **Nutshell Series** from Round Hall is an accessible review of key principles, concepts and cases. Nutshells are both the ideal introductory text, and the perfect revision aid.

- **Administrative Law** by Matthew Holmes
- **Company Law** – 3rd edition by Catherine McConville
- **Contract Law** by Fergus Ryan
- **Constitutional Law** – 2nd edition by Fergus Ryan
- **Criminal Law** – 3rd edition by Cecilia Ní Choileáin
- **Equity and Trusts** – 2nd edition by Miriam Dowling
- **Employment Law** – 2nd edition by Dorothy Donovan
- **EU Law** by Matthew Holmes
- **Evidence** by Ross Gorman
- **Family Law** by Louise Crowley
- **The Irish Legal System** by Dorothy Donovan
- **Land Law** – 2nd edition by Ruth Cannon
- **Succession Law** by Karl Dowling and Robert Grimes
- **Tort** – 2nd edition by Ursula Connolly

NUTCASE TITLES

Round Hall Nutcases are written to give you the key facts and principles of **important cases** in core legal subject areas. Straightforward, no-nonsense language makes Nutcases an easy way to understand and learn key cases.

- **Criminal Law** by Majella Walsh
- **Evidence** by Neil Van Dokkum
- **Tort** – 2nd edition by Val Corbett

EXAM FOCUS TITLES

The series is especially designed to support students in the weeks coming up to exams by providing a unique tutorial approach to answering questions.

- **Criminal Law** by Sarah Carew

LEGAL SKILLS TITLES

The Legal Skills Series helps students master the essential legal and research skills needed to succeed in their studies and in their future careers.

- **How to Think, Write and Cite: Key Skills for Irish Law Students**, 2nd edition by Jennifer Schweppe, Rónán Kennedy and Lawrence Donnelly

NUTSHELLS

EU Law

FIRST EDITION

by

MATTHEW HOLMES
BCL, LLM (KCL)
Barrister-at-Law (King's Inns, Bar of Northern Ireland, Middle Temple)

ROUND HALL
THOMSON REUTERS

Published in 2017 by
Thomson Reuters Ireland Limited
(Registered in Ireland, Company No. 416940. Registered Office
and address for service 43 Fitzwilliam Place, Dublin 2)
trading as Round Hall.

Typeset by Carrigboy Typesetting Services

Printed and bound in the UK by
CPI Group (UK) Ltd, Croydon, CR0 4YY

ISBN 978–0–41406–099–9

A catalogue record for this book is available from the British Library.

For my family and in
loving memory of Mamó McElwee

Preface

Despite previous promises, it turns out that this is my follow on to *Administrative Law Nutshell*, rather than *Dating Secrets of the Third Reich*, as once suggested. Sadly, chapters like "What the Luftwaffe can Teach you about Wingmen" will probably never come to pass.

There are many people who should be thanked for their assistance. In particular, my proofreaders who were of invaluable assistance. Whilst I absolutely could have written it without them, it would have been a much poorer work without them. I owe a debt to Donough Farrell, Beatrice Vance, Tom L. Power, Niall O'Huiginn, Sara-Jane Smyth, Aoife McMahon, Declan Moran, Tommy O'Donoghue, Michael McCormack and in particular Cian O'Brien. Their work is top notch and any errors or omissions are my own.

Others who must be thanked include my parents for their boundless patience and support; Dr Mary Rogan, without whom this text would not exist; my colleagues at the Bar and in the Office of the Refugee Applications Commissioner; the staff and law schools at DIT, King's College London and UCD; Frieda Donohue and everyone at Round Hall; and, of course, my friends, in particular Sean, Tracey, Vinny, Colm, Eoin and Dermot.

This book represents the law as I understand it as of July 2016.

Contents

Table of Cases

IRELAND

EU

(Alphabetically)

(Numerically)

Table of Legislation

Bunreacht na hÉireann

Irish Statutes

Statutory Instruments

European Treaties, Conventions, Regulations, Directives and Decisions

Treaties and Conventions

Regulations

Directives

Decisions

Recommendations

Introduction to European Union Law

1

Introduction

EU law is rarely any law student's favourite subject. There are a number of reasons for this: while it is important and effective, it is also dense, complex and, frankly, boring. International agreements governing a supranational institution made up of almost 30 countries, with a history well over half a century long, are never going to be simple. Cases which turn on international chemical tax regulations cannot hope to be as interesting as cases on cannibalism, carbolic smokeballs or snails in bottles. What's more, EU law is very different to most other subjects as it largely comes from a civil law background rather than the common law, with which Irish students are more familiar. Many may also hold preconceived political opinions about the EU. Once students get over the initial difficulties, however, it becomes easier to grasp and more interesting, and opinions on the topic and the EU itself may change.

This text hopes to help make this complex area of law easier to understand. It is made up of 13 chapters which can be divided into two parts. The first nine chapters deal with the foundations of EU law and the last four deal with the substantive law of the EU—the principles known as "the four freedoms of EU law", protected by the internal market and contained in art.26 of the Treaty on the Functioning of the European Union. The four freedoms are the free movement of people, goods, capital, and services. This chapter will look at the history of the EU and how it has developed legally. It will then look at how EU law is cited, the differences between EU judgments and common law judgments, and various areas where EU law applies. It will also consider some of the difficulties that changes in EU law may create for students, before ending with a list of useful online resources.

The History of the EU

Europe lay in ruins in the aftermath of World War Two. France and Germany had a history of mutual hatred and millions had been killed in wars involving both countries over territory and resources. It is a fact sometimes overlooked that the event used to finally unify Germany was the 1871 Franco-Prussian War. Both countries had been devastated economically by World War Two and, with the Cold War looming, the future of Europe looked bleak.

On 9 May 1950, the French Foreign Minister, Robert Schuman, proposed a community to integrate the coal and steel industries of Europe—these having been previously used in the manufacturing of war munitions. This was the brainchild of Jean Monnet, a senior French civil servant. The proposal was made in a famous speech known as the "Schuman Declaration". Its aim was to make war between France and Germany "not merely unthinkable, but materially impossible".

On the basis of the Schuman Declaration, France, West Germany, Italy, Belgium, the Netherlands and Luxembourg signed the Treaty of Paris in 1951, creating the European Coal and Steel Community (ECSC). This community had a number of institutions which would evolve into the institutions that make up the European Union today. There was the Common Assembly (now the European Parliament), the High Authority (now the European Commission) and a single court called the Court of Justice of the European Coal and Steel Communities (which evolved into the Court of Justice of the European Union—the General Court and the European Court of Justice).

In 1957, these countries took a step closer towards the European Union when they signed the Treaty of Rome. This treaty is still in force today and is now called the Treaty on the Functioning of the European Union (TFEU). It is one of the core treaties making up the EU. This treaty created the European Economic Community (EEC), or "Common Market". The idea behind the Common Market was that people, goods and services should be able to move freely across borders within the EEC as if it was one country. On the same day, they signed the Euratom Treaty which created a market for nuclear power in Europe.

The Common Agricultural Policy (CAP) was introduced in 1962. The Member States had endured a period of severe food shortages following the war. The CAP gave Member States joint control over food production and, as a result, farmers across the EEC were paid the same price for their produce and given subsidies. The policy was a success but has led to claims of over-production, and so-called "Wine Lakes" and "Butter Mountains".

In 1963 and 1964, the Court of Justice handed down the two most important judgments in European law: *Van Gend En Loos* (C-26/62) [1963] E.C.R. 1 and *Costa v ENEL* (C-6/64) [1964] E.C.R. 585. *Van Gend En Loos* gave rise to the doctrine of direct effect, which allows citizens to rely on European law in the courts of Member States. *Costa v ENEL* gave rise to the doctrine of supremacy, which states that European law is superior to the law of Member States.

The first enlargement of the Member States came about in 1973 when Ireland, the UK and Denmark joined. Norway rejected joining at the same time. In Ireland, 83.1 per cent of the voters voted in favour of the third amendment to Bunreacht na hÉireann which allowed the country to become a Member State. Ireland would have joined sooner had Charles de Gaulle not blocked the UK, our main trading partner, from joining on a number of occasions.

The European Regional Development Fund was set up in 1974. Its purpose is to address regional economic imbalances by transferring money from rich to poor regions to improve infrastructure. It now accounts for one third of all EU spending.

On 7–10 June 1979, citizens had the opportunity to directly elect their representatives in the European Parliament for the first time. Before then, Members of the European Parliament (MEPs) were delegated by national parliaments.

The second enlargement brought the number of Member States to double figures when Greece joined in 1981. Greece had been ruled by a military regime and was not a democracy until 1974. Greece's rival, Turkey, applied to join in 1987 but at the time of writing is not yet a Member State.

The European flag was adopted by the European Parliament in 1983 and became the official emblem of the European Communities in 1985. It is not mentioned in the Treaties. It is made up of a blue background with 12 gold stars. The 12 stars never stood for the number of Member States; at the time it was adopted, there were only 10 Member States.

The third enlargement took place in 1986 when Spain and Portugal joined, bringing the number of Member States to 12. Until the 1970s, they had been military dictatorships under Francisco Franco and Antonio Salazar, respectively, but they had since become democracies. 1986 also saw the signing of the Single European Act (SEA). This was the first major amendment to the Treaty of Rome. It aimed to create a single market in Europe and it changed the way in which legislation is created. In Ireland, the case *Crotty v An Taoiseach* [1987] I.R. 713 was taken because of the SEA. This case says that the doctrine of supremacy does not require Ireland to ratify the SEA. *Crotty* is the reason that every time there is an amendment to the European Treaties, there must be a constitutional referendum in Ireland in order to ratify it.

The year 1989 saw the fall of the Berlin Wall. The following year East and West Germany were reunited and the Eastern parts of Germany joined the Union.

The second major change to the Treaties came with the signing of the Maastricht Treaty in 1992. This treaty is now called the Treaty on European Union (TEU) and, along with the TFEU, is one of the primary treaties that make up EU law. The European Community officially became the European

Union under this Treaty. It also led to the creation of the single currency, the euro. The TEU created what was referred to as the "pillar structure" of the European Union, where European power was divided into three pillars; the European Communities, the Common Foreign and Security Policy, and Judicial Co-operation in Criminal Matters. The TEU forms the basis of EU law; it sets out the general principles of the EU's purpose, how the institutions of the EU are governed and the rules on external, foreign and security policy.

The fourth enlargement of the EU took place when Austria, Finland and Sweden joined in 1995. The EU now had 15 Members. 1995 was also the year that the Schengen Agreement first took effect. Travellers of any nationality could now travel between all of the countries within the Schengen area without having to show a passport at the national borders as border controls were abolished. Originally, the Schengen area was made up of seven countries, now it is made up of 26. Ireland is not a Member of the Schengen Agreement.

The Treaty of Amsterdam increased the powers of the EU. It was signed in 1997, amending the Treaty of Maastricht and introducing changes which allowed for the expansion of the Union.

The euro currency arrived in 2002. It is used as currency in 19 Member States. Member States can issue their own coins, but bank notes are issued by the European Central Bank. Coins have designs to show the State from which they were issued; Irish coins feature a harp. Bank notes are illustrated with architectural designs which are intended to evoke architecture found within the EU. They are not based on real structures; however, the Dutch town of Spijkenisse subsequently built seven bridges based on the designs on the banknotes. The Vatican has its own monetary agreement with the EU which allows it to use the euro.

The Nice Treaty was signed in 2001. It amended the structure of the EU to allow for enlargement by Central and Eastern European States. It was voted on twice by Irish citizens after it was rejected in the first referendum, and was finally ratified in 2002.

The fifth enlargement took place in May 2004. Ten countries joined the EU: Cyprus, the Czech Republic, Estonia, Hungary, Latvia, Lithuania, Malta, Poland, Slovenia and Slovakia. This is the single largest accession to the EU, both in terms of population and in the number of countries. In October of that year, the 25 EU Member States signed a Treaty establishing a European Constitution. It had to be ratified by all Member States before it could come into force and was rejected in both France and the Netherlands in referendums in 2005.

The sixth enlargement took place in January 2007 when Bulgaria and Romania joined the EU, bringing the number of Member States to 27. In December of that year, the Member States signed the Treaty of Lisbon, which amended the previous Treaties. It was designed to make the EU more democratic, efficient and transparent. It amended both the Treaty of Rome and the Treaty of Maastricht, which were now renamed the Treaty on the Functioning of the European Union and the Treaty on European Union. As with the Treaty of Nice, Ireland voted on this twice, having rejected it on the first occasion. It also gave equal legal standing to the Charter of Fundamental Rights of the European Union, which enshrines rights for EU citizens into law. The Lisbon Treaty also abolished the three pillars structure which was introduced by the Treaty of Maastricht. It entered into force on 1 December 2009.

In 2012, the European Citizens' Initiative came into operation. It gives citizens the ability to propose the creation of a law to the European Commission. The EU was awarded the Nobel Peace Prize in 2012 "for over six decades [having] contributed to the advancement of peace and reconciliation, democracy and human rights in Europe".

Croatia joined the EU in the seventh enlargement in 2013. The EU now comprises 28 Member States.

On 23 June 2016, the UK voted to leave the EU by a majority of 51.9 per cent. This was an event known as "Brexit". Membership of the EU had long been a source of controversy in the UK. This was an advisory referendum, and at the time of writing the British Government has yet to invoke art.50 TEU, which will formally begin the departure process. If it does so, this will be the first time a Member State leaves the EU. Some politicians in other Member States have indicated that they would like to hold similar referendums on leaving the EU. The fall-out of Brexit remains to be seen.

EU Citations

Judgments of the Court of Justice of the European Union

Judgments of the Court of Justice of the European Union (CJEU) differ from those from common law countries, about which students may be more knowledgeable. They are different both in their style and the way in which they are handed down. CJEU judgments are majority decisions and are read out at public hearings. The author of the judgment is not named and no dissenting opinions or obiter dicta are given. CJEU judgments have their own numbering system rather than the common law citation style. Judgments which come from the Court of Justice cases have the letter "C" (e.g. Case C-1/99) and judgments which come from the General Court cases have the Letter "T" (e.g. Case T-1/99) from the former name of this court, the French *Tribunal de première instance*. The first number is the case number and the second is the year when the proceedings began. "Opinions" and "Rulings" of the CJEU, as opposed to "Cases", are numbered separately (e.g. Opinion 1/99). Opinions of an Advocate General have the number of the case in which they were given. A number of cases, particularly cases in the area of free movement of goods, are referred to by nicknames. This may be because there are a lot of cases with the same parties (for example, in the free movement of goods cases, there are a number between the Commission and Italy, such as "The Italian Art Treasures case" or "The Italian Statistics case"), or because their facts are memorable (for example, *Commission v France* (C-265/95) "Angry Farmers") or because the title of the case is quite difficult (for example, *Rewe-Zentral AG v Bundesmonopolverwaltung für Branntwein* (C-120/78) "Cassis de Dijon").

Citation of a case

- *Commission v Ireland* (C-494/01) [2005] E.C.R. I-3331

Elements of the citation

- *Commission v Ireland* = names of the parties
- C = a Court of Justice case
- 494 = case number
- 01 = year it was added to the Register
- [2005] = year of decision/publication
- E.C.R. = where the text can be found (*European Court Reports*)
- I-3331 = Section I, starting on page 3331

When citing an opinion of an Advocate General, add a comma and the words "Opinion of A.G. [name]" after the case citation, e.g. *Commission v Ireland* (C-494/01) [2005] E.C.R. I-3331, "Opinion of A.G. Geelhoed".

The layout of the case is also different to the layout used in a common law judgment. It is usually presented in three parts. First, the summary of judgment appears, followed by the report for the hearing drawn up by the judge assigned to the case. This contains the facts and procedure. Secondly, the opinion of the Advocate General, although this does not form an official part of the report. Finally, the grounds for the judgment is set out in numbered paragraphs, and the ruling of the court. EU law and judgments are available in all of the official languages of the EU. Many textbooks make reference to just the first part of the citation, e.g. *Commission v Ireland* (C-494/01), and omit the second part, e.g. [2005] E.C.R. I-3331. This approach will be used in the body of this textbook.

Citation of EU Legislation

In 2015, the EU law citation style was harmonised. The citation of EU legal acts is now laid out in the format (Domain) YEAR/NUMBER. The Domain indicates what the case deals with, e.g. Euratom or CFSP (Common Foreign and Security Policy).

Examples

Regulation (EU) 2016/1
Directive (EU) 2016/1
Council Decision (CFSP) 2016/1
Decision (Euratom) 2016/1 of the European Parliament.

Changes to EU Law to be Aware of

EU law has changed and developed significantly over the decades. Students may come across these changes if they read older textbooks or articles. The area where they are most likely to come across these changes are in judgments. The EU has only been called the European Union since the signing of the Treaty of Maastricht in 1992. Students may find references to "the Community" in older judgments—this can now be taken as meaning the Union. Another significant change to EU law that students will come across is the change to the numbering of the articles of the Treaties. The treaty articles were recently changed in 2010 as part of the Lisbon Treaty; for example, judicial review under art.263 TFEU was previously under art.230 TEC. Students should be aware of this when reading judgments from before 2010 as the numbering of articles will be different.

The European Court of Human Rights

It is a common misconception that the European Court of Human Rights (ECHR) is an EU institution or is in some way connected to the EU. It is not, and should not be confused with the Court of Justice of the European Union (CJEU). This is an easy mistake to make as all of the Members of the EU are signed up to the European Convention on Human Rights, and signing up is a condition for joining the EU. The ECHR sits in Strasbourg, whereas the CJEU sits in Luxembourg. The European Coal and Steel Community chose not to adopt the European Convention on Human Rights due to France's rejection of the closely linked Defence Community Treaty in 1954. The European Union itself is not signed up to the European Convention on Human Rights, although the Lisbon Treaty gave the Union the power to do so. The EU is not bound by the rulings of the ECHR, but the CJEU gives the ECHR "special significance" as a "guiding principle" in its case law. Prior to the enactment of the Charter of Fundamental Rights, the main instrument for the protection of human rights which the CJEU drew upon was the European Convention on Human Rights. In *Kremzow v Austria* (C-299/95), it was held that the European Convention on Human Rights has a special significance which the CJEU draws inspiration from when dealing with fundamental human rights and their position in EU law.

The European Economic Area, the Customs Union and Schengen

A number of non-EU Member States are part of three different groupings: the European Economic Area (EEA), the European Customs Union and the Schengen Area.

The EEA is an area where the four freedoms of EU law—the free movement of goods, persons, services and capital—is in force. This includes all of the Member States of the EU (except Croatia, the newest EU Member State) as well as Iceland, Lichtenstein and Norway. This trade will be covered by the law of the EU, into which the non-Member States have no input.

The EU Customs Union is an area with no customs on goods travelling between countries. It is made up of the Member States as well as Turkey, Andorra, Monaco and San Marino.

The Schengen Area is an area with common passport controls and visa entry requirements. Once you are in the Schengen Area, you do not need to show your passport to enter another Schengen country. Schengen is made up of the EU Member States—excluding Ireland and England (both of which opted out), Croatia, Romania and Bulgaria—as well as non-Member States Switzerland, Luxembourg, Norway and Iceland.

At the time of writing, Britain is still an EU Member State and has yet to begin its negotiations to leave the EU. It is unclear where it will stand in relation to these areas once it leaves.

Useful Websites and Resources

- The official website of the EU: *http://europa.eu/*

- The websites of the institutions of the EU: *http://www.europarl.europa.eu/addresses/institutions/websites.htm*
- The website of the Court of Justice (this is very useful for finding cases): *http://curia.europa.eu/*
- *Official Journal of the European Union*: *http://publications.europa.eu/official/index_en.htm*
- EUR-LEX for European Union Law: *http://eur-lex.europa.eu/en/index.htm*
- An English-language version of the Consolidated Treaties: *http://eur-lex.europa.eu/LexUriServ/LexUriServ.do?uri=OJ:C:2010:083:FULL:EN:PDF*
- A video by the European Commission containing a recording of the Schuman Declaration: *https://www.youtube.com/watch?v=pzhpA7_-1oA*
- A search tool to find the social media accounts of the European Institutions: *https://europa.eu/european-union/contact/social-networks_en.*

2 Institutions of the European Union

Introduction

Article 13 TEU lists seven institutions as being the institutions of the European Union. They are: the European Parliament, the European Council, the Council of the European Union, the European Commission, the Court of Justice of the European Union (CJEU), the European Central Bank and the Court of Auditors. They are governed by arts 13–19 TEU. The powers of the European Central Bank and the Court of Auditors are found in Pt 6 of the TFEU. Collectively, these institutions make up the EU. When looking at the powers of these institutions, it can be seen that their powers are designed so that they interact with one another; for example, the Commission can take Member States before the CJEU or propose legislation which is adopted by the Parliament and the Council.

What do they do?

Three of the institutions hold the executive and legislative power of the Union. The Council of the European Union represents governments of the Member States, the Parliament represents citizens of the Union, and the Commission represents interests of the EU itself. Together, these three bodies have the power to create legislation and manage the EU's budget of approximately €155 billion.

The CJEU is the judicial branch of the Union; it ensures that EU law is interpreted uniformly and consistently in all Member States and cases for breaches of EU law are brought before it. The European Council sets the EU's overall political direction. The Central Bank and the Court of Auditors manage the EU's finances.

The make-up of these institutions has evolved since the European Coal and Steel Community, as have their powers and abilities.

The European Parliament

The European Parliament represents the people of Europe. It is the only EU institution whose members are directly elected by the citizens of Europe. The powers and duties of the European Parliament are found in art.14 TEU, as well as in arts 223–234 TFEU. Originally, it was only an assembly with advisory and supervisory powers, but it has grown in importance over the decades. It is based in Strasbourg and Brussels. The Parliament shares power with the Council, including the power to propose legislation and to decide on the EU budget. It elects the President of the Commission and supervises the work of the Commission and other institutions. It can vote to have the entire Commission replaced, but has only done so once (during the Commission of Jacques Santer in 1999). Prospective Member States are approved for EU Membership by the Parliament.

The European Parliament is made up of 750 seats, plus the President. The number of seats per country varies. Representation is proportional, with a minimum of six seats per country and maximum of 96; Ireland has 11 seats. Members of the European Parliament (MEPs) do not sit by country; instead, they sit by groups based on political beliefs, e.g. the Christian Democrats or the Nordic Green Left. MEPs serve a five-year term. The Parliament elects its own President and 14 Vice Presidents for two-and-a-half-year periods.

The European Council

The European Council defines the EU's overall political direction and priorities. The powers and duties of the European Council are found in art.15 TEU. It should not be confused with the Council of the European Union which is governed by art.16 TEU. The European Council is not one of the EU's legislating institutions, so it does not negotiate or adopt EU laws. It is, however, central to the EU's decision-making process as it sets the EU's policy agenda. Article 15(1) states:

> "The European Council shall provide the Union with the necessary impetus for its development and shall define the general political directions and priorities thereof. It shall not exercise legislative functions."

The European Council is made up of the heads of government of the EU Member States and the President of the Commission. It meets twice every six months. Unless the Treaties say otherwise, the European Council's voting is done by consensus. All important developments within the EU are considered by the European Council. It exercises powers of appointment and appoints the President of the European Central Bank and the High Representative of the Union for Foreign Affairs and Security Policy. It also proposes a candidate for President of the European Commission to the European Parliament. The European Council can make the decision to suspend membership of Member States for serious breaches under art.7 TEU and it sets the criteria for new states to join under art.49 TEU. Article 50 sets out the procedure by which Member States leave the EU; they are required to notify the European Council of their intention to leave under this procedure.

The Council of the European Union

The Council of the European Union is the institution which represents the interests of the Member States' Governments. It is the main political institution of the EU and is governed by art.16 TEU. It should not be confused with the European Council despite their similar names. It was previously known as the Council of Ministers. The Council of the European Union shares its power with the European Parliament. Article 16(1) TEU states:

> "The Council shall, jointly with the European Parliament, exercise legislative and budgetary functions. It shall carry out policy-making and coordinating functions as laid down in the Treaties."

The Council of the European Union is made up of ministers from each Member State. Whenever the Council meets, the relevant ministers from each Member State with responsibility for that subject area will attend. Council meetings are arranged by subject matter; for example, a meeting on the subject of agriculture and fisheries will have the ministers for agriculture from every Member State. It meets in 10 configurations (prior to Lisbon there were 99 configurations!). The presidency of the Council is held by Member States for six months on a rotational basis.

The Council of the European Union has quite a number of powers, the most important of which are those budgetary and legislative powers it shares with the Parliament. The Council has the power of final say in many areas; it must give approval to any of the Commission's legislative proposals before they can become law. It can delegate decision-making power to the Commission and has the power to request the Commission to undertake studies or submit legislative proposals. It works with the Parliament on the Union's budget. The Council decides the salaries of a number of the most important figures in the EU. The Council can take other institutions before the Court of Justice for failure to fulfil their EU law obligations. It frames the EU's common foreign and security policy and deals with international agreements on the EU's behalf. It also co-ordinates Member States policies in areas such as education, culture, youth and sport, employment policy, and economic and fiscal policies. The Council uses a number of different voting systems depending on what is being voted on; sometimes, a unanimous vote must be reached, while a majority is required on other occasions. The Council is assisted by the Committee of Permanent Representatives ("Coreper") which carries out tasks assigned to it by the Council and prepares the Council's agenda.

THE EUROPEAN COMMISSION

The European Commission is the executive body of the European Union. It is responsible for the day-to-day running of the EU as well as proposing legislation, implementing decisions and upholding the EU Treaties. The powers and responsibilities of the European Commission can be found in art.17 TEU and its headquarters are in Brussels. It is seen as the most federal of the EU institutions and has been called the "Watchdog" of the Treaties. In this way, its members look after the best interests of the EU as a whole. The Commission was set up to act as an independent supranational authority separate from governments. Article 17 states:

> "1. The Commission shall promote the general interest of the Union and take appropriate initiatives to that end. It shall ensure the application of the Treaties, and of measures adopted by the institutions pursuant to them. It shall oversee the application of Union law under the control of the Court of Justice of the European Union. It shall execute the budget and manage programmes. It shall exercise coordinating, executive and management functions, as laid down in the Treaties. With the exception of the common foreign and security policy, and other cases provided for in the Treaties, it shall ensure the Union's external representation. It shall initiate the Union's annual and multiannual programming with a view to achieving interinstitutional agreements.
>
> 2. Union legislative acts may only be adopted on the basis of a Commission proposal, except where the Treaties provide otherwise. Other acts shall be adopted on the basis of a Commission proposal where the Treaties so provide."

The European Commission has a number of powers. One of its jobs is to propose legislation which is then adopted by the European Parliament and the Council. It enforces EU law, at times taking Member States to court in the CJEU for breaches of EU law; it manages and implements EU policies and budget; it represents the Union to the outside world, for example, by negotiating trade agreements between other countries or with organisations such as the World Trade Organization (WTO), and it also investigates countries applying for EU membership.

The Commission's make up

There is one European Commissioner from every Member State. They work independently from the interests of the Member States. A new team of Commissioners is appointed every five years. First, the candidate for President of the Commission is proposed to the European Parliament by the European Council. The European Commission President is then elected by the European Parliament by a majority of its members. Following this, the President-elect selects the other members of the Commission, on the basis of suggestions made by Member States. The Commission as a whole needs the Parliament's consent. Once the commissioners are appointed, they are given a portfolio by the President of the Commission and are responsible for that area. A member of the Commission or the High Representative of the Union for Foreign Affairs and Security Policy will resign if the President requests they do so. The president has seven vice presidents.

Article 9D5 of the Lisbon Treaty reduced the number of Commissioners from one per Member State to the equivalent of two thirds of the Member States (i.e. 18 or 19 Commissioners). The Treaty also permitted the European Council to unanimously alter this number. This Treaty was originally rejected by the people of Ireland in a referendum. As a result, the European Council gave the undertaking that if Ireland adopted the Treaty in another referendum, it would exercise its power to alter the number of Commissioners so that Ireland and every other Member State would keep its Commissioner. The Lisbon Treaty was subsequently passed by the Irish people and the European Council has kept its word, but it still has the power to alter the number of Commissioners.

The Court of Justice of the European Union

The Court of Justice of the European Union (CJEU) is the judicial body of the European Union. Its job is to ensure that EU law is interpreted and applied uniformly and consistently in all Member States, to rule on breaches of EU law and to settle legal disputes between Member States and the EU institutions. It sits in Luxembourg and is modelled on the French *Cour de Cassation*. It has a number of powers and doctrines to make sure that EU law is treated in the same way in all Member States and these will be discussed throughout this book. It was originally established in 1952 as a single court called the Court of Justice of the European Coal and Steel Communities. The CJEU is governed by art.19(1) TEU, which states:

> "The Court of Justice of the European Union shall include the Court of Justice, the General Court and specialised courts. It shall ensure that in the interpretation and application of the Treaties the law is observed. Member States shall provide remedies sufficient to ensure effective legal protection in the fields covered by Union law."

The CJEU has been one of the main driving forces behind the development of EU law. A number of doctrines of EU law such as supremacy and direct effect were developed by the CJEU and were not originally found in the Treaties. It is unrelated to the European Court of Human Rights, which sits in Strasbourg, but it does give the case law of that court "special significance" as a "guiding principle". The CJEU is made up of two separate courts: the Court of Justice and the General Court. There was previously a third court known as the EU Civil Service Tribunal which ruled on disputes between the European Union and its staff. It ceased to exist in September 2016 when its jurisdiction was transferred to the General Court.

The most important court of the CJEU is the Court of Justice. The Court of Justice has one judge per Member State. These judges are appointed for a term of six years, which can be renewed, and they elect the President of the Court who sits for three years. The Court of Justice is assisted by a number of "advocates-general" who present impartial opinions on the cases before the Court. This position comes from the French legal tradition; they have the same background and status as judges and serve for equal terms. They are not inferior to judges and their responsibilities can be found in art.252 TFEU.

The General Court was introduced to help the Court of Justice deal with the large number of cases brought before it. The General Court deals with cases brought by private individuals, companies and cases relating to competition law. It was previously known as the Court of First Instance. Most of the cases looked at in this book come from the Court of Justice rather than the General Court.

Types of cases

The five most common types of cases before the CJEU are:

- Preliminary rulings: when national courts ask the Court of Justice to interpret a point of EU law;

- Enforcement actions: brought by the European Commission against Member States for breaching EU law;
- Annulment actions: brought against EU laws thought to violate the EU Treaties or fundamental rights;
- Actions for failure to act: brought against EU institutions for failing to take actions required of them; and
- Direct actions: brought by individuals, companies or organisations against EU decisions or actions.

These types of actions will be analysed in later chapters.

One of the main influences on how the CJEU operates is the French legal tradition; this is reflected by the fact that the working language of the CJEU is French. As a result, the CJEU operates differently to common law, with which Irish students and lawyers might be more familiar. For example, there is no equivalent position to Advocate General in common law, cases can be televised, and judgments are handed down differently.

How cases are heard

A judge and an advocate general are assigned to each case that comes before the CJEU. This judge is called the "judge-rapporteur" and is in charge of the case and how it progresses. Cases before the Court have two stages: a written stage and an oral stage.

Written stage

First, the parties to the case submit written statements to the judge-rapporteur. Member States and institutions can make observations on the cases at this stage; Ireland, for example, has been known to make observations in immigration cases involving other Member States. The judge-rapporteur then writes a summary of these statements and the case's legal background and decides if the oral stage and an advocate general are needed.

Oral stage

The second stage is the public hearing. Depending on how complicated or important the case is, this can take place before a panel of three, five or thirteen judges or in front of the whole court. At the hearing, lawyers from both sides put their case to the judges and the Advocate General, who can question them. The Advocate General then gives his or her opinion. After this, the judges discuss the case together and give their judgment.

Advocates General are only required to give their opinion on the case if the Court believes that it raises a new point of law. The Court does not have to follow the Advocate General's opinion, although, in practice, generally does so. This opinion is given after the hearing.

The hearings in the General Court are similar, except that most cases are heard by three judges and there are no Advocates General.

THE EUROPEAN CENTRAL BANK

The European Central Bank (ECB) is the central bank of the 19 Member States which use the euro. It governs monetary policy of the Eurozone and is governed by arts 127–133 TFEU. Under art.282 TFEU, it will be consulted on all proposed Union acts and may give an opinion on matters which fall inside its responsibility. It forms the European System of Central Banks (ECSB) together with the central banks of the Member States. The primary objective of the ECB is to maintain price stability within the eurozone. The ECB conducts foreign exchange operations, takes care of the foreign reserves of the ECSB and defines and implements the monetary policy for the eurozone. The ECB has, under art.128 TFEU, the exclusive right to authorise the issuance of euro banknotes. Member States can issue euro coins, but the amount must be authorised by the ECB beforehand. This is why coins bear symbols showing which state they come from, whereas notes have no such identifying marks.

THE COURT OF AUDITORS

The Court of Auditors is the guardian of the EU's finances. This institution monitors the revenue and expenditure of the EU. It is governed by arts 285–287 TFEU. While not a court in the traditional sense, as it is not a judicial body, the Court of Auditors is an accounting body. It is based in Luxembourg and looks after the interests of EU taxpayers. The Court of Auditors is made up of one member from each EU Member State, who sits for a period of six years, which can be renewed. They elect one of their own members to be president for three years. The primary role of the Court of Auditors is to check if the budget of the European Union has been implemented correctly and that EU funds have been spent legally and with sound management. In doing so, the Court checks the paperwork of those handling any income or expenditure of the Union and carries out spot checks. They examine the finances of the EU, its bodies, offices and agencies. The Court of Auditors has no jurisdiction to enforce its control measures or to investigate suspicions of irregularity arising from its investigations. Rather, its main weapon is publicity; it sends on an annual report to the other EU institutions. It can deliver opinions at the request of another institution if it is consulted on legislative proposals.

3 Sources and Types of EU Law

Sources of EU Law

There are two main sources of EU law: primary law and secondary law. Primary law is made up of the Treaties which lay down the legal framework of the European Union. Secondary law covers legal instruments which are made pursuant to these Treaties, such as Regulations and Directives. This chapter will look at the various types of EU law as well as how EU law is made.

Primary EU Law

Primary law is the most important source of law in the European Union. It is made up of the EU Treaties. These Treaties play a similar role to EU law as the Constitution plays to Irish law. They are binding agreements between all of the Member States of the EU. The most important treaties are:

- the Treaty on European Union (TEU)
- the Treaty on the Functioning of the EU (TFEU)
- the Charter of Fundamental Rights in the EU
- the Treaty establishing the European Atomic Energy Community
- Protocols and annexes to these Treaties
- Member States' accession treaties.

While it may appear that there a number of treaties, the most important are the TEU and the TFEU, as these are the two core Treaties. As a result, these two will be referred to a lot more frequently than any of the other Treaties in this text. The TEU summarises the institutions and focuses on principles of democracy and human rights, while the TFEU describes the role, the policies and the operation of the EU in finer detail. Of these two, the TFEU will be referred to most often in this book.

These Treaties are at the top of the European legal system; they set out the ground rules for how the EU works. They give the objectives of the EU and the powers of its institutions. They control how power is divided between the

EU and the Member States and outline the decision-making process. Every action taken by the EU is founded on these Treaties. The Member States have agreed to surrender some of their sovereignty to give powers to the supranational instruction that is the EU. Amending these Treaties requires the agreement of all Member States. The Member States surrender their power in various competences: legislative, executive and judicial. Article 1 TEU states:

> "By this Treaty, the HIGH CONTRACTING PARTIES establish among themselves a EUROPEAN UNION, hereinafter called 'the Union' on which the Member States confer competences to attain objectives they have in common."

The EU can only act within the powers, known as competences, conferred upon it by these Treaties. These powers are voluntarily surrendered by the Member States, the EU has no power of its own, and competences not conferred on the EU remain with the Member States. For example, the EU has exclusive competence within the area of the Customs Union; only it can make law for the Customs Union. On the other hand, it has no competence for court procedure in the Member States; it cannot create legal procedure in the Member States.

Dualism/Monism

Ireland is a dualist state. Dualist states do not automatically recognise international law as part of their domestic law. This means that international treaties are not part of Irish law unless incorporated by the Oireachtas. Countries which are not dualist states are known as monist states. Holland, for example, is a monist state. They recognise international law as being part of their own law automatically.

In *Crotty v An Taoiseach* [1987] I.R. 713, the Supreme Court said there was a power to review the constitutionality of treaties signed by the state and that the government could be prevented from signing up to international agreements which would be contrary to the Constitution. This is why there are referenda every time Ireland adopts a new European Treaty which alters the purpose or powers given to the EU, as opposed to it simply being adopted by the government, which is the case in other Member States.

Secondary EU Law

EU legislation makes up the secondary sources of EU law; the institutions of the EU have the power to make legislation. There are five main types of secondary

EU law. They are Regulations, Directives, Decisions, Recommendations and Opinions. This can be contrasted with Irish law which has only two types of secondary law: statutes and statutory instruments. These laws are made pursuant to the Treaties and come from the principles and objectives set out in them. Article 288 TFEU governs these types of laws; it states:

> "To exercise the Union's competences, the institutions shall adopt Regulations, Directives, Decisions, Recommendations and Opinions.
>
> A Regulation shall have general application. It shall be binding in its entirety and directly applicable in all Member States.
>
> A Directive shall be binding, as to the result to be achieved, upon each Member State to which it is addressed, but shall leave to the national authorities the choice of form and methods.
>
> A Decision shall be binding in its entirety. A Decision which specifies those to whom it is addressed shall be binding only on them.
>
> Recommendations and Opinions shall have no binding force."

They will be analysed individually in turn here.

Regulations

Regulations are used to legislate for the whole European Union and are, perhaps, the strongest form of legislation the EU can create. When they come into effect they immediately become the law in all Member States. Regulations under art.288 have three main elements. First, they have "general application", which means that they apply to all Member States. Secondly, they are "binding in [their] entirety". This means that they are binding in relation to the method as well as the result to be achieved. Thirdly, "directly applicable" signifies that they are automatically applicable on Member States and do not need to be transposed into national law. By contrast, when Directives are created, Member States are required to adapt the law into their own laws. This is called transposition; the Member States transpose the Directive into their law. This requirement does not exist with a Regulation—once it is created, it is the law. Direct application gets rid of the need for dualist states to take transposing measures before a Regulation takes effect in its members. The EU has such an abundance of Regulations that if they all had to be individually adopted into national law, the system would grind to a halt, so this is done for efficiency. With Regulations, the law immediately becomes enforceable in all Member States simultaneously. In *Racke v Hauptzollampt Mainz* (C-98/78), it was held that:

> "The unity and uniform application of Community Law require that, save as otherwise expressly provided, a Regulation should enter into force on the same date in all the Member States, regardless of any delays which may arise in spite of efforts to ensure rapid distribution of the Official Journal throughout the Community."

When they come into force, Regulations override all national laws dealing with the same subject matter and subsequent national legislation must be consistent with the Regulation.

In *Leonesio v Ministero dell'agricoltura e foreste* (C-93/71), it was held that Regulations have direct effect and can therefore be relied upon in court. In *Variola v Amministrazione dela Finanze* (C-33/73), it was held that Member States could not try and make Regulations look like their own law or try to hide the fact they are EU Law. In *Producteurs of fruit v Council* (C-16 and 17/62), it was clarified that Regulations apply not to a limited group of people, but to everyone. In *Maher v Minister for Agriculture and Food* [2001] 2 I.R. 139, which concerned the regulation of milk quotas, Keane C.J. held that as the milk quota scheme was a creation of the EU, one had to look to the Treaties of the European Union and not to any Irish legislation in order to determine the principles and policies which underlay it.

Directives

Directives are one of the most important forms of EU legislation along with Regulations. They are the most commonly used form of EU legislation. They make sure that EU law is the same in all Member States whilst at the same respecting the diversity of national legal traditions and government structures. Instead of ensuring that EU law is exactly the same in every Member State like Regulations do, Directives instead ensure that the effect of EU law is the same in every state. Different states might have different ways of ensuring that EU law has the same effect.

Directives differ from Regulations in two main ways. First, they are not necessarily addressed to all Member States. They can be addressed to all Member States, some specific Member States or even just one Member State. Directive 2016/343 on the presumption of innocence, for example, does not include Ireland. Secondly, they are binding to the specific result that is to be achieved, but leave choice as to the ways and means to the Member States. This gives the EU flexibility. As Regulations are parachuted directly into Member States law, a lot of effort goes into creating them and making sure that they are correct, as Member States cannot alter them. If this was the only way of creating legislation, then the legislative process would work very slowly. As a result, Directives are used for the bulk of EU law-making as they give more flexibility.

Directives stipulate the result that is to be achieved by the Member State(s) to which they are addressed and a specified time-frame (usually two years) within which that result is to be achieved. Individual Member States are free to choose the methods by which they transpose the Directive into their own law. If the laws of a Member State already comply with this obligation, then the state must only keep its existing laws in place. There is a lot of case law on what happens if an EU Directive is not transposed in time, or if it is transposed badly. This will be looked at later in different parts of this book. States must refrain during the implementation period from adopting measures that could compromise the result prescribed by the Directive: see *Inter-Environnement Wallonie* (C-129/96).

In Ireland, the main way by which Directives are transposed is by statutory instrument. Section 3 of the European Communities Act 1972 allows government ministers to implement EU measures through statutory instruments. This also allows the minister to vary, alter or repeal any inconsistent piece of Irish legislation however they see fit; the European Communities Act 2007 grants similar powers. In *Meagher v Minister for Agriculture* [1994] 1 I.R. 329, the Supreme Court noted that statutory instruments were the only practical way of transposing EU law into Irish law "possibly in a great majority of cases". This is because there are so many Directives to be implemented each year that the Oireachtas would grind to a halt if it required a statute for each one. The Oireachtas could not keep pace with the changes in EU law and Ireland would quickly fall into default of its obligations to transpose Directives in time. Subsequently, in *Maher v Minister for Agriculture* [2001] 2 I.R. 139, the Supreme Court clarified that statutory instruments are not always appropriate for transposing EU law. Where Directives leave the Member State discretion to create principles and policies, then an Act of the Oireachtas is required. The Supreme Court in *National Asset Management Agency v Commissioner for Environmental Information* [2015] IESC 51 emphasised the need to appreciate the extent and terms of an EU Directive while identifying the different concepts of administrative law and public law throughout the Member States. O'Donnell J. noted:

> "The problem of interpretation posed in this case calls to mind the observations of the Caliph of Baghdad on the burning of the library of Alexandria ... if it contained nothing that was not in the Koran it was superfluous and if it contained something different it was dangerous."

In *Eircom Ltd v Commission for Communications Regulation* [2007] 1 I.R. 1, McKechnie J. observed that the Supreme Court is obliged to interpret national Regulations which "were passed in order to incorporate ... Directives into national law, in a manner, so far as is possible, in conformity with the Directives".

Decisions

The next type of legal act are Decisions. In some cases, the institutions may be responsible for implementing the Treaties and Regulations of the EU. This is only possible if they can make binding measures; these measures are known as Decisions. Article 288 TFEU says a Decision is binding in its entirety. Decisions are different to Regulations in that they specify who they are binding on, whereas Regulations are binding on everyone. They are different to Directives in that they are binding, whereas Directives only give a result that is to be achieved.

A Decision can be binding on Member States, legal persons or individuals and each Decision will specify on whom it is binding. Legal persons are generally companies but also include states, government ministers and the EU itself. Decisions are not binding on those to whom they are not addressed. In one high profile example when the Commission issued a Decision imposing a fine on Microsoft for its abuse of a dominant market position for web browsers, the only body bound was Microsoft. There are many instances where the use of Decisions is required by the Treaties. For example, art.105(2) TFEU says that when competition law is infringed, "[t]he Commission shall record such an infringement in a reasoned Decision".

Recommendations and Opinions

Recommendations and Opinions are not legally binding; however, the use of these two instruments may help clarify matters in a formal way. They provide guidance on the interpretation and content of EU law. In *Grimaldi v Fonds des Maladies Professionnelles* (C-322/88), it was held that national courts were

> "bound to take Community Recommendations into consideration in deciding disputes submitted to them, in particular where they clarify the interpretation of national provisions adopted in order to implement them or where they are designed to supplement binding EEC measures."

A Recommendation allows the institutions to make their views known and to suggest a line of action or course of behaviour without imposing any legal obligation on the party to whom they are addressed. For example, in cases where a law of a Member State causes a distortion of competition in the European internal market, the Commission may recommend appropriate measures to the Member State to avoid this distortion (art.117(1) TFEU).

An Opinion, on the other hand, gives an assessment of a situation or development in Member States or the Union. It can prepare the way for subsequent acts which are legally binding. It can also be a prerequisite for proceedings in the CJEU. It can be issued by the main EU institutions, the Committee of the Regions and the European Economic and Social Committee. When laws are being made, the committees give Opinions from their specific regional or economic and social viewpoint.

Recommendations and Opinions are not legally binding. Their real importance is that they carry persuasive political weight. By creating Recommendations and Opinions, the treaty drafters felt that those receiving Recommendations and Opinions would voluntarily comply with them because of the importance of the institutions.

How EU Law is Made

Ordinary legislative procedure

EU Regulations and Directives are made by the Commission, the Parliament and the Council. Article 294 TFEU outlines the ordinary legislative procedure. This is the EU's standard legislation-making procedure, where the European Parliament approves EU legislation with the Council. The European Parliament or the Council of the European Union may request the Opinion of the Commission throughout the procedure, which the European Commission may also deliver on its own initiative. This used to be known as "co-decision".

Legislative proposals

First, the European Commission will create proposals for new legislation and then it will submit it to the Parliament and the Council. The Commission presents legislation on its own initiative but can also be requested to submit proposals by the Parliament and the Council. There is also the citizens' initiative which allows EU citizens to ask the Commission to come up with proposals for new legislation. This requires one million signatures from citizens from at least seven Member States. The Commission publishes around 70–80 draft legislative proposals per year.

The proposal is submitted to the Parliament and the Council and the ordinary legislative process is carried out in a number of stages known as readings.

First reading

At the first reading, the Parliament will adopt its position and communicate it to the Council of the European Union. If the Council approves the Parliament's position, the act will be adopted in the wording which corresponds to the Parliament's position.

If the Council does not approve the Parliament's position, it shall adopt its position at first reading and communicate it to the Parliament. It will inform the Parliament fully of the reasons which led it to adopt its position and the Commission will do the same. Around 30 per cent of legislation is adopted at the first reading.

Second reading

If, within three months of this, the Parliament:

(a) approves the Council's position or hasn't taken a decision, the act will be adopted in the wording which corresponds to the Council's position;
(b) rejects the Council's position, the proposed act shall be deemed not to have been adopted;
(c) proposes amendments to the Council's position, the amended text will be forwarded to the Council and Commission, which will deliver an Opinion on those amendments.

If, within three months of receiving the Parliament's amendments, the Council:

(a) approves all those amendments, the act will be adopted;
(b) does not approve all the amendments, the President of the Council, in agreement with the President of the Parliament, shall convene a meeting of the Conciliation Committee within six weeks.

Around 50 per cent of legislation is adopted at the second reading.

Conciliation

The Conciliation Committee is made of Council members and an equal number of members representing the European Parliament. It has the task of reaching agreement on a joint text within six weeks of being convened. The Commission takes part in its proceedings and shall take all necessary steps with a view to reconciling their positions. If, within six weeks of being convened, the Conciliation Committee does not approve the joint text, the proposed act will not be adopted. If the Conciliation Committee approves a joint text, the European Parliament and the Council each have six weeks to adopt the act in question in accordance with the joint text. If they do not do so, the proposed act is not adopted. When a legislative proposal fails at the conciliation stage, the Commission frequently redrafts the proposal in a more acceptable form and presents it again.

Special legislative orocedures

The Treaties have provision for special legislative procedures to be used in certain areas. These are governed by art.289(2) TFEU. Special legislative procedures replace the former consultative, co-operation and assent procedures. The objective is to simplify the EU's decision-making process by making it clearer and more effective. In practice, under these procedures, the Council is the sole legislator. There are two types of procedure: consent and consultation.

Consent

Under the consent procedure, the European Commission makes a proposal which must be either rejected or accepted by the Parliament. The Parliament has the power to accept or reject a legislative proposal by an absolute majority vote, but does not have the power to amend it. This legislative procedure is used when new legislation on combating discrimination is being adopted; where there are breaches of fundamental rights; and with decisions relating to the structure of the EU, its budgets, membership, withdrawal from the Union and relations with other countries.

Consultation

Under the consultation procedure, the Council of the European Union adopts a legislative proposal after the Parliament has submitted its Opinion on it. In this procedure, the Parliament may approve, reject or propose amendments to a legislative proposal. The Council is not legally obliged to take the Parliament's Opinion into account but it must not take a Decision without having received it (*Isoglucose* (C-138/79)). Failing to consult with the Parliament is a grounds for the annulment of the legislation. This procedure is used in several areas, such as internal market exemptions and competition law.

Delegated and implementing acts

Delegated acts

Article 290 TFEU allows legislative acts to delegate to the Commission the power to adopt non-legislative acts to supplement or amend certain non-essential elements of that piece of legislation. The limits of this power must be found within the act. The "essential area" of the act is reserved for the act itself and cannot be delegated. The European Parliament and the Council can revoke the delegation and it can only enter into effect if they do not object within a specified time limit. Only the Commission can have this power delegated to it.

An example where delegated acts might be appropriate would be to add new non-essential rules to a legislative act. This allows the legislative bodies to concentrate on policy objectives without having to get into detailed technical debates.

Implementing acts

The Member States adopt all measures of national law necessary to implement EU laws. Where EU laws need to be implemented uniformly throughout the Member States, art.291 TFEU gives powers to implement the act to the Commission. Articles 24 and 26 TEU give implementing powers to the Council.

Rules for how implementing acts are to be adopted are set out in a dedicated Regulation: reg.182/2011. This Regulation allows the Member States to control the use of these implementing powers. They do so by the use of several committees and the process is therefore known as "comitology".

4 Direct Effect, Indirect Effect and State Liability

Introduction

Direct effect, indirect effect and state liability are three separate doctrines that have been developed through the case law of the Court of Justice to protect the EU rights of individuals before their national courts. Direct effect, along with some of the doctrines in the next few chapters, will deal with the relationship between EU law and the law of Member States. Direct effect allows you to rely on EU law in the courts of Member States; indirect effect allows the courts of Member States to interpret their own law in light of EU law; and state liability allows you to sue Member States for their failure to implement EU law. These principles will be analysed in turn below.

Direct Effect

The direct effect of EU law is a one of the most important principles in EU law. This is the principle that EU law creates rights which can be relied upon in the courts of the Member States. Direct effect did not exist in the Treaties, but developed from the case law of the Court of Justice. In particular, it developed from the judgment of *Van Gend en Loos Nederlandse Administratie der Belastingen* (C-26/62).

Van Gend en Loos

Van Gend en Loos is acknowledged as being one of the most important, and possibly the most famous case in European Union law. It arose out of tariffs imposed on urea-formaldehyde imported from West Germany to the Netherlands. In this case, the Court of Justice held that

> "the Community constitutes a new legal order of international law for the benefit of which the states have limited their sovereign rights, albeit within limited fields and the subjects of which comprise not only Member States but also their nationals. Independently of the legislation of Member States, community law therefore not only imposes

> obligations on individuals but is also intended to confer upon them rights which become part of their legal heritage. These rights arise not only where they are expressly granted by the treaty, but also by reason of obligations which the treaty imposes in a clearly defined way upon individuals as well as upon the Member States and upon the institutions of the Community."

This means that the provisions of the Treaties were capable of direct effect, i.e. they could be relied upon by individuals in the courts of Member States.

Criteria for direct effect

According to the decision in *Van Gend en Loos*, the criteria for direct effect are that the EU law must:

- be clear and precise;
- be a negative, rather than positive obligation;
- be unconditional;
- contain no reservation on the part of the Member State; and
- not be dependent on any national implementing measure.

These criteria were then developed by subsequent case law. *Van Gend en Loos* only dealt with treaty provisions and did not deal with other types of EU law. *Leonesio v Ministero dell' Agricolura delle Foreste* (93/71) held that Regulations can have direct effect and *Van Duyn v Home Office* (41/74) held that Directives can also have direct effect. In *Kücükdeveci* (C-555/07), it was even held that the general principles of the European Union can have direct effect. In *Reyners v Belgium* (2/74), the Court set out what are now the criteria for direct effect:

- the provision must be clear and unambiguous;
- the provision must be unconditional; and
- its operation must not be dependent on any further action on the part of the Member State.

Vertical and horizontal direct effect

There are two types of direct effect: vertical direct effect and horizontal direct effect. The difference between them is based on who the case is being taken against. Vertical direct effect arises in cases taken against Member States, while horizontal direct effect arises in cases between private individuals. This distinction is important as Directives generally cannot be horizontally directly effective. The state has more power when it comes to the law than individuals and is therefore above them, this is why it is referred to as vertical direct effect. Cases taken by individuals are called horizontal because they are at the same level of law-making power. Vertical direct effect concerns the relationship between EU law and national law—specifically, the state's obligation to comply with EU law, thereby enabling citizens to rely on it in actions against the state or against public bodies.

Defrenne v Sabena (43/75) is the case which established horizontal and vertical direct effect. Ms Defrenne took a case against Sabena Airlines, the then national Belgian airline, on the grounds of what is now art.157 TFEU; which provides that "the principle of equal pay for male and female workers for equal work". She was forced to retire at 40, men were not. As a result, she had less pension entitlements. The Court of Justice held that the prohibition on discrimination between men and women applies not only to the action of public authorities, but also contracts between individuals. This means that the articles of the Treaties could be relied upon in direct effect cases, not just against the state, but also against other individuals.

Horizontal direct effect concerns the relationship between private individuals. If a certain provision of EU law is horizontally directly effective, citizens are able to rely on it in actions against each other. Directives are usually not horizontally directly effective, meaning they cannot be relied upon against other private individuals, just against the state. This stems from the judgment in *Marshall v South West Hampshire area Health Authority Teaching* (152/84). In this case, a woman was dismissed when she reached the retirement age of 60, whereas the retirement age for men was 65. Certain provisions of the Treaties and legislative acts such as Regulations are capable of being directly enforced horizontally. The Court here held that "a Directive may not of itself impose obligations on an individual and that a provision of a Directive may not be relied on as such against such a person". It also held that "it is necessary to prevent the State from taking advantage of its own failure to comply with Union law".

An example of this in practice in Ireland is *Albatros Feeds Ltd v Minister for Agriculture* [2007] 1 I.R. 221. There the Supreme Court noted:

> "Directives do not have automatic direct effect. They depend for their effect on national implementing legislation. While there was a well-established line of case law permitting direct effect to be allowed for Directives as *against* a Member State or its emanations, the converse did not and could not apply. The first respondent cannot rely on the direct effect of article 8."

Emanations of the state

There is an exception to the rule that Directives cannot be relied upon horizontally. This is the "emanation of the state" exception which comes from *Foster v British Gas* (C-189/89). This case allows Directives to have horizontal direct effect against individuals who are emanations of the state. In this case, Mrs Foster had to retire from her job at British Gas when she was 60 years old, while men could continue working until they were 65. British Gas was a nationalised industry at the time. She and four other women claimed this was unlawful discrimination on grounds of sex, which was against the Equal Treatment Directive (Directive 76/207). Directives in principle only bind the Member State to which they are addressed, therefore Mrs Foster needed to show that British Gas was part of the state in order to make a claim against them. She argued this point on the basis that the board members of British Gas were appointed by the Secretary of State, who could also issue to the board various directions and instruments. The board was also required to submit reports to the Secretary of State. The Court held that a Directive could be relied on against organisations or bodies which were subject to the authority or control of the State or had special powers beyond those which result from the normal rules applicable to relations between individuals. The emanation of the state exception has been found to include employees of health authorities, as in *Marshall*; employees of local government bodies, *Fratelli Constanzo SpA v Commune di Milano* (C-103/88); and a police chief, *Johnston v Chief Constable of the RUC* (C-222/84).

Direct effect and different types of EU law

Direct effect applied from the beginning to primary EU law, meaning the Treaties. Article 288 TFEU is silent on whether or not it applies to secondary EU law. The case law subsequent to *Van Gend en Loos* clarified that it does; however, it depends on the type of act:

- Regulations always have direct effect. Article 288 TFEU specifies that Regulations are directly applicable in the Member States and *Leonesio* determines that this means that they have direct effect. The Court of Justice clarified in the judgment of *Politi* (43/71) that Regulations have both horizontal and vertical direct effect.
- Directives do not have automatic direct effect. They depend on national implementing legislation to have effect. However, in certain cases, the Court of Justice recognises the direct effect of Directives in order to protect the rights of individuals. The Court in *Van Duyn* held that a Directive has direct effect when its provisions are unconditional and are sufficiently clear and precise. In that case, a Dutch woman wanted to travel to the UK to

work for the Church of Scientology. The British Government had a policy of refusing immigration permission to scientologists because they believed scientology was harmful to mental health. The Court in *Becker v Finanzamt Münster-Innenstadt* (8/81) found that for a provision of a Directive to have direct effect, it must be "unconditional and sufficiently precise". In *Ratti* (148/78), it was held that a Directive can only have direct vertical effect and it is only valid if the Member States have not transposed the Directive by the deadline. Directives do not have horizontal direct effect and therefore cannot be used against individuals other than emanations of the state.

- Decisions have direct effect against those to whom they are addressed as art.288 states: "A decision shall be binding in its entirety upon those to whom it is addressed." It was held in *Grad* (9/70) that they are therefore capable of having direct effect. In *Hansa Fleisch* (C-156/91), it was held that:

> "Where a decision addressed to the Member States contains precise and unconditional provisions which must be implemented within a specified period, the provisions may be relied on by individuals as against a Member State only if that State fails to implement the decision before the expiry of the period prescribed or implements it in time, but incorrectly."

- Regarding international agreements, in *Demirel* (12/86), the Court of Justice recognised the direct effect of certain agreements in accordance with the same criteria identified in *Van Gend en Loos*.
- Opinions and Recommendations do not have legal binding force. As a result, they do not have direct effect.

Direct effect in Ireland

Direct effect of EU law has been recognised in Ireland since before we joined the EU. Section 2 of the European Communities Act 1972 recognises that the law of the EU "shall be binding on the State and shall be part of the domestic law thereof under the conditions laid down in [the treaties]". This automatically makes EU law part of Irish law. It gives individuals the right to rely on EU law in an Irish court and for it to give them legal rights they would not otherwise have. The leading judgment on direct effect in Ireland is that of Fennelly J. in *Dellway Investments Ltd v NAMA* [2011] 4 I.R. 1. There, he found a Commission Decision did not meet the criteria for direct effect.

Indirect Effect

What happens if a Member State fails to implement a Directive or implements it badly? There, the doctrine of indirect effect (also known as harmonious interpretation) arises. Indirect effect is where national courts are required to interpret national law in line with an unimplemented or badly implemented Directive, instead of ignoring national law in preference to the Directive, which is what happens when direct effect is used.

Indirect effect arises from the failure of a Member State to implement a Directive, either correctly or at all, but where direct effect does not apply. In *Von Colson and Kamann v Land Nordrhein-Westfalen* (14/83), a group of German women were denied employment in the German prison service because of their gender. They sought to rely on art.6 of the Equal Treatment Directive, but it did not have direct effect as it was not sufficiently precise to guarantee them a specific remedy of appointment to a post. The Court held that national courts should interpret national law in line with the Directive, "in so far as it is given discretion to do so under national law". The Court in *Von Colson* found that national courts are the branch of government responsible for the discharge of EU law obligations. It encouraged national courts to supplement domestic legislation, which does not on its face provide a remedy, by reading it as complying with the Directives requirement to provide a real and effective remedy.

Von Colson dealt with a situation where a Member State had failed to implement a Directive correctly. In *Marleasing v La Comercial Internacional de Alimentacion* (C-106/89), the CJEU widened indirect effect to situations where a Member State had not implemented the Directive at all. There it was held that the courts of the Member States have a duty to interpret national legislation in light of unimplemented Directives. This judgment also confirmed that an unimplemented Directive could be relied upon to influence the interpretation of national law in a case between individuals. In addition to this, it clarified that indirect effect applies to legislation which predates the Directive and it applies to all national law, not just law which specifically relates to the Directive.

This principle is now found in the TEU; art.4(3) states:

> "The Member States shall take any appropriate measure, general or particular, to ensure fulfilment of the obligations arising out of the Treaties or resulting from the acts of the institutions of the Union."

The CJEU has interpreted this as meaning that national courts are under a duty to interpret national law consistently with EU law, so far as it is possible to do so, regardless of whether or not the Directive has direct effect. Indirect effect is a principle on the interpretation of national law; its use is left to the discretion of the national courts.

Operation of direct and indirect effect and state liability

Indirect effect works in tandem with direct effect. Where a Directive has direct effect, national courts must ignore domestic law that conflicts with it. Where a Directive does not have direct effect, the national courts must interpret domestic law consistently with the Directive. In *Dominguez* (C-282/10), the CJEU advised national courts how these doctrines should be used. First, the national court must interpret domestic law in the light of the wording and the purpose of the Directive in order to achieve results sought by that Directive. However, such an interpretation cannot serve as the basis for an interpretation *contra legem* (i.e. it cannot be interpreted in such a way that goes against the law). Secondly, if that interpretation is impossible, the national court must determine whether the Directive has direct effect. The result of this is then disregarding any national provisions of law which conflict with the Directive. Where the case is taken against an individual and direct effect of the Directive therefore cannot be relied upon, the injured party can rely only on *Francovich and Bonifaci* (C-6/90; C-9/90) in order to obtain compensation due to the fact that the domestic law does not comply with EU law.

Limits of indirect effect

(i) Where national legislation clearly conflicts with the relevant Directive

Under *Marleasing*, all national law must be interpreted in line with EU law, but only "so far as possible". Indirect effect cannot apply where national legislation clearly conflicts with the relevant Directive; there are limits to how far the meaning of language can be stretched when it is being interpreted. Words cannot be interpreted as meaning something they do not. In *Wagner Miret v Fondo De Garantia Salarial* (C-334/92), the CJEU introduced the *contra legem* principle here. The Spanish state had failed to introduce a Directive on workers' rights. The CJEU held that it was not possible to interpret national legislation, which excluded higher management employees from compensation, consistently with a Directive which did not exclude them. This was against the natural meaning of the words used in the legislation.

(ii) Where indirect effect would impose criminal liability

In *Public Prosecutor v Kolpinghuis Nijmegen BF* (80/86), a Dutch firm was prosecuted for stocking adulterated mineral water which was in breach of an EU Directive. The Dutch authorities tried to use provisions of an unimplemented Directive; the implementation period had expired and the Netherlands should have implemented it, but had not. The Court held that to rely on indirect effect to impose criminal liability would breach the principles of legal certainty and non-retroactivity.

In *Criminal proceedings against Luciano Arcaro* (C-168/95), Mr Arcaro was prosecuted for industrial discharge of dangerous substances, specifically the chemical cadmium, into the aquatic environment. Under the Italian implementing legislation he was not guilty, under the Directive he was. The CJEU held that indirect effect cannot impose criminal liability.

Indirect effect in Ireland

In *Nathan v Bailey Gibson Ltd* [1998] 2 I.R. 262, the Chief Justice held that the Supreme Court

> "is in the same position and under the same obligations as any other national court to interpret the provisions of (the Anti-Discrimination Pay Act, 1974), as far as possible, in the light of the wording and the purpose of the Directive in order to achieve the result pursued by the Directive."

In *Albatros Feeds v Minister for Agriculture and Food* [2007] 1 I.R. 221, Fennelly J. observed:

> "[It is] perfectly clear that the Court is under an obligation to interpret national law, so far as possible, in the light of the Community provisions it is designed to implement."

In *Eircom Ltd v Commission for Communication Regulations* [2006] IEHC 138, Irish legislation was interpreted by the High Court in the light of the Directives that the legislation purported to implement to allow a broader right of appeal. In *Smith v Meade* [2009] IEHC 99, Peart J. applied indirect effect and supremacy of EU law to determine that exclusions clauses in insurance contracts were void.

State Liability

State liability is a way to overcome the limits of direct and indirect effect. Originally, the CJEU said there was no requirement for Member States to create new remedies. In *Rewe Handelsgescellshaft Nord* (C-158/80), it was held that "[i]t was not intended to create new remedies in the national courts to ensure the observance of Community law other than those already set down in national law." However, *Francovitch and Bonifaci v Italy* (C-6/90) introduced the remedy of damages for state liability. The doctrine of state liability means that Member States can be liable for a breach of their EU obligations. If somebody suffers a loss because a State breached its EU law obligations, they can sue for damages.

In *Francovitch and Bonifaci*, Italy had failed to transpose Directive 80/987 in time (the same Directive from *Wagner Miret*). This Directive dealt with workers' protection in the event that their employer became insolvent. The plaintiffs were owed money by their employers but Italy had not implemented the Directive and so there was no guarantee scheme for their wages. They argued that the Directive was directly effective and, in the alternative, that the Italian state was liable in damages for its failure to transpose the Directive in time. The Directive was held not to be directly effective as it was insufficiently clear and it did not identify the body who would guarantee the workers' wages; however, the court held:

> "It is a principle of Community law that the Member States are obliged to make good loss and damage caused to individuals by breaches of Community Law for which they can be held responsible".

Three conditions were laid down in order to succeed in such a case:

1. The result prescribed by the Directive should entail the grant of rights to the individuals.
2. It should be possible to identify the contents of those rights on the basis of the provisions of the Directive.
3. There must be a causal link between the breach of the state's obligation and the loss and damage suffered by the injured parties.

Before this case, there had been a successful art.258 TFEU enforcement action against Italy in relation to this Directive; however, the Court of Justice does not require that there be a successful enforcement action in order for the state to be found liable for damages. It was also held that the Directive was not directly effective. It is clear from the subsequent case law that a plaintiff is not obliged to rely on direct effect where this is possible but can instead sue the state in damages (even if the provision is not directly effective). This is a different mechanism and the plaintiff has a choice over which one he or she uses. This case dates to two years before the EU had the power to fine Member States for failure to comply with Court of Justice rulings, which was introduced by the Maastricht Treaty in 1992.

State liability for breaches of EU law other than failure to transpose a Directive

In subsequent cases, the Court of Justice has held that damages are available against Member States for breaches of EU law other than failing to transpose Directives. This stems from the landmark joined cases of *Brasserie du Pêcheur v Germany* and *R. v Secretary of State for transport, Ex p. Factortame* (C-46-93; C-48-93). There it was held that the state could be liable in damages for enacting legislation contrary to EU law. These cases had different facts but similar issues. *Factortame* involved legislation which prevented Spanish fishermen fishing from UK ports. *Brasserie de Pêcheur* involved a challenge to the Germany beer laws when French beer did not conform to them. It was held that state liability was a "necessary corollary of ... direct effect".

Brasserie du Pêcheur and *Factortame* can be distinguished from *Francovich* in that they involved a state action which did not comply with the Treaties, rather than a failure to implement a Directive. However, the Court of Justice ignored this difference and held that the conditions laid down in *Francovich* could apply to actions as well as omissions in respect of any EU law, as long as the law gave rights to individuals. The Court held that the right to compensation for breach of EU law existed even where the breach was caused by an act of the national legislature. The Court noted that Member States could not "make it impossible or extremely difficult to obtain effective reparation for loss or damage resulting from a breach of Community law." The Court also gave examples of what would be unacceptable restrictions. The test for state liability is now:

1. The rule of law infringed must have been intended to confer rights;
2. The breach must be sufficiently serious; and
3. There must be a direct link between the state's obligation and the injured parties' injuries.

This test is very similar to the *Francovich* test; only the second of these criteria differs. The Court gave a list of factors as follows, which can be used to determine whether or not a breach is sufficiently serious.

> "[T]he clarity and precision of the rule breached, the measure of discretion left by that rule to the national or Community authorities, whether the infringement and the damage caused was intentional or involuntary, whether any error of law was excusable or inexcusable, the fact that the position taken by a Community institution may have contributed towards the omission and the adoption and retention of national measures or practices contrary to Community law.

... On any view, a breach of Community law will be sufficiently serious if it has persisted despite a judgment finding the infringement in question to be established, or a preliminary ruling or settled case law of the Court on the matter from which it is clear that the conduct in question constituted an infringement."

In *R. v HM Treasury, Ex p. BT* (C-392/93), it was held that a Member State could be held liable in damages for incorrectly implementing a Directive. In *R. v Minister for Agriculture, Fisheries and Food, Ex p. Hedley Lomas (Ireland) Ltd* (C-5/94), it was held that a Member State could be liable for damages for an administrative decision contrary to EU law. This obligation applies to all state authorities, regardless of whether they are legislative, administrative or judicial. In *Kobler v Austria* (C-224/01), the Court held that a Member State could be liable for the incorrect application of EU law by a court of last resort.

State liability in Ireland

This issue arose in *Tate v Minister for Social Welfare* [1995] 1 I.R. 418 which was taken in relation to the non-implementation in Ireland of the Equal Treatment Directive between men and women. Carroll J. held that the failure to implement a Directive on time was a wrong belonging to a new legal order and that the nature of the wrong was similar to a breach of the constitutional duty. She also noted that:

> "Even though the State has wriggled for ten years in its efforts to avoid paying the same to women as to men, in view of the very large sums involved, I do not intend to add any element of punitive or exemplary damages."

In *Ogieriakhi v Ireland* [2016] 1 I.L.R.M. 504, the applicant had originally been awarded damages of over €100,000 for breach of his free movement rights, but this was overturned by the Court of Appeal.

Supremacy

5

Introduction

The principle of supremacy guarantees that European Union law is superior to national laws. It is also referred to as the precedence or primacy principle. It is one of the most fundamental doctrines of EU law and is arguably the most important. Supremacy was developed to avoid differences between the way the Member States interpret and apply EU law. EU law is superior to the national laws of all Member States, even constitutional laws. This means that national law cannot amend or revoke EU law and, in the event that they clash, it is EU law which takes priority. Due to the principle of supremacy, EU citizens are protected in the same way by EU law no matter which Member State they are in. It applies to all EU Acts with legal binding force.

Like the doctrine of direct effect, the supremacy of EU law did not originate in the Treaties, but has developed from and by the case law of the CJEU. It can now be found in Declaration 17 of the Treaty of Lisbon which states:

> "The fact that the principle of primacy will not be included in the future treaty shall not in any way change the existence of the principle and the existing case-law of the Court of Justice."

The doctrine of supremacy is one of the more controversial aspects of European Union law and was frequently mentioned in national debates on the EU; however, it is worth noting that its existence predates Ireland and England's entry into the EU by almost a decade. The reason for this rule is obvious; EU law would be of little use if the laws of Member States could amend, revoke or overrule it. If this were the case, it would not be uniformly applied throughout the EU, if it were even applied at all. The EU would therefore be unable to function.

Costa v ENEL

The doctrine of supremacy originates from the decision in *Costa v Enel* (C-6/64). This issue did not arise in the earlier case of *Van Gend en Loos* (C-26/62), as Holland is a monist state and had therefore already accepted the supremacy of EU law. However, the Court held that that the Community constituted "a new legal order of international law for the benefit of which the States had limited their sovereign rights". *Costa* is one of the two most important cases in EU law and it arose out of an unpaid bill for less than a euro. Flaminio Costa was an Italian who owned shares in Edison Volta, an electricity company which was being nationalised. He opposed this and, in protest, refused to pay his electricity bill. He was sued by the newly-created state electricity company, ENEL. In his defence, he argued that the nationalisation of the electricity industry violated EU law. Italy, like Ireland, is a dualist state. The Italian State argued that the nationalising law had come into effect after the Act ratifying the European Treaties and that, therefore, the nationalising law should take legal priority. This was referred to the CJEU. The Court of Justice held:

> "The law stemming from the Treaty, an independent source of law, could not, because of its special and original nature, be overridden by domestic legal provisions, however framed, without being deprived of its character as Community law and without the legal basis of the Community itself being called into question.
>
> The transfer by the States from their domestic legal system to the Community legal system of the rights and obligations arising under the Treaty carries with it a permanent limitation of their sovereign rights, against which a subsequent unilateral act incompatible with the concept of the Community cannot prevail."

This means that EU law therefore has precedence or supremacy over national laws. If a national law is contrary to a European Union law, Member States' authorities must apply the EU law and no new national legislation may be introduced unless it is compatible with EU law. National law is neither rescinded nor repealed, but its binding force is suspended.

Development of the Doctrine

The doctrine of supremacy was developed by Court in later cases. In *Internationale Handelsgesellschaft* (C-11/70), the Court clarified that supremacy means that EU law also applies to fundamental rules of Member State law such as constitutional law. In this case, there was a conflict between a Regulation and provisions of the German Constitution. There had been an attempt to nullify an EU Regulation as it breached the principle of proportionality enshrined in the German Constitution. The Court held that the validity of EU law cannot be challenged on grounds of national law, even if that is a violation of fundamental human rights provisions in a Member State's Constitution. This means that EU law is superior even to constitutional law.

In *Simmenthal II* (C-106/77), a company from Italy claimed that a public health inspection fee under a 1970 Italian law for importing beef from France was contrary to two Regulations from 1964 and 1968. Here it was held that there is a duty on national courts to set aside provisions of national law which are incompatible with EU law. The Court emphasised that this applies regardless of whether or not the national legislation existed before the EU legislation or if it was enacted afterwards. It held:

> "[A] national court ... is under a duty to give full effect to those provisions, if necessary refusing of its own motion to apply any conflicting provision of national legislation, even if adopted subsequently, and it is not necessary for the court to request or await the prior setting aside of such provision by legislative or other constitutional means."

It is clear from this judgment that any law of a Member State which is incompatible with EU law cannot stand, regardless of when it was introduced. The Court has clarified in *Ministero delle Finanze v IN.CO.GE.'90 Srl* (C-10–22/97) that *Simmenthal* did not mean that if a national law is incompatible with EU law it does not render that law non-existent, but instead national courts have to "dissapply" that law.

In *Marleasing SA v La Comercial Internacional de Alimentacion SA* (C-106/89), it was held that there is a duty on national courts to interpret and apply national law in such a way as to avoid a conflict with EU law so far as possible. In *Fratelli Constanzo* (C-103/88), it was held that "[e]very court and organ of the state is obliged to apply the doctrine of supremacy", and this was confirmed in Ireland in *M.A.P. v Refugee Applications Commissioner* [2015] IEHC 647. In *Factortame II* (C-213/89), the Court of Justice held that, due to the doctrine of supremacy,

> "[c]ommunity law must be interpreted as meaning that a national court which, in a case before it concerning Community law, considers that the sole obstacle which precludes it from granting interim relief is a rule of national law must set aside that rule."

In *Melloni* (C-399/11), it was held that an EU Framework Decision prevails over the Spanish Constitution. Mr Melloni was an Italian businessman who was prosecuted for bankruptcy fraud and tried to escape justice by fleeing Spain. A Spanish court authorised his extradition to Italy but at the same time released him on bail. Mr Melloni fled and never appeared before the Italian court. He was convicted in his absence, although his lawyers were present. This was upheld by all levels of the Italian judiciary. He was later arrested by the Spanish police and the Italians sought a warrant for his extradition. He claimed this was in breach of his right to a fair trial. The EU Framework Decision on the European Arrest Warrant was found there to be superior to the Spanish Constitution.

In joined cases *Kadi & Al Barakaat International Foundation v Council and Commission* (C-402/05 P and C-415/05), it was made clear that EU law takes precedence over all other claims of international law and any decisions of international tribunals such as the European Court of Human Rights.

Scope of the Principle

EU law is absolutely supreme over all national laws. Therefore, it applies to all European acts with a binding force, regardless of whether or not they are primary or secondary legislation. In addition, all national acts are subject to this principle regardless of what type of act they are or where they come from. The judiciary is also subject to the precedence principle, i.e. the case law of Member States should respect EU case law. The Court of Justice has ruled that national constitutions should also be subject to the precedence principle. It is, therefore, a matter for national judges not to apply the provisions of a constitution which contradict European law.

There is one limit to the doctrine of supremacy, which is when it comes up against the doctrine of res judicata. Res judicata is the legal doctrine which says that once a case has been ruled upon and all avenues of appeal have been exhausted, it is finished and cannot be taken again. Otherwise, people would take the same cases over and over again and the courts would be unable to function. In *Kapferer* (C-234/04), the CJEU held:

> "In that regard, attention should be drawn to the importance, both for the Community legal order and national legal systems, of the principle of res judicata. In order to ensure both stability of the law and legal relations and the sound administration of justice, it is important that judicial decisions which have become definitive after all rights of appeal have been exhausted or after expiry of the time-limits provided for in that connection can no longer be called into question.
>
> Therefore, Community law does not require a national court to disapply domestic rules of procedure conferring finality on a decision, even if to do so would enable it to remedy an infringement of Community law by the decision at issue."

This means that the doctrine of supremacy does not require national courts to disapply their own rules of procedure in order to review and set aside a final judicial decision if that decision is contrary to EU law.

Responsibility for Ensuring Compliance with Supremacy

As with the principle of direct effect, the Court of Justice is responsible for ensuring that supremacy is complied with. Its rulings impose penalties on Member States who infringe the doctrine of supremacy, on the basis of the various remedies provided for by the Treaties, in particular proceedings for failing to fulfil EU law obligations. It is also the job of national judges to ensure that supremacy is complied with. If there is any doubt as to how supremacy is to be implemented, judges can use the preliminary ruling mechanism. In *Factortame*, the Court of Justice indicated that national courts, as part of a preliminary ruling on the validity of a national law, must immediately suspend the application of this national law until such time as the Court of Justice gives its recommended solution and the national court gives its ruling on the substance of the issue.

Supremacy and Irish Law

The Third Amendment of the Constitution of Ireland explicitly provides for the supremacy of EU law in Ireland. Article 29 of the Constitution deals with international relations. Article 29.4.6° now provides:

> "No provision of this constitution invalidates laws enacted, acts done or measures adopted by the State, before, on or after the entry into force of the Treaty of Lisbon, that are necessitated by the obligations of membership of the European Union referred to in subsection 5° of this section or of the European Atomic Energy Community, or prevents laws enacted, acts done or measures adopted by—
>
> i the said European Union or the European Atomic Energy Community, or institutions thereof,
>
> ii the European Communities or European Union existing immediately before the entry into force of the Treaty of Lisbon, or institutions thereof, or
>
> iii bodies competent under the treaties referred to in this section,
>
> from having the force of law in the State."

Henchy J., writing extra-judicially in an article "The Irish Constitution and the EEC" (1977) D.U.L.J. 20, said of this: "It is as if the people of Ireland had adopted Community law as a second but transcendent Constitution." This was cited by the High Court in *McGrath Limestone Works v Mayo Co. Council* [2014] IEHC 382. Supremacy of EU law in Ireland is also provided for by s.2 of the European Communities Act 1972, as amended by s.3 of the European Union Act 2009. This states:

> "The following shall be binding on the State and shall be part of the domestic law thereof under the conditions laid down in the treaties governing the European Union:
> (a) the treaties governing the European Union;
> (b) acts adopted by the institutions of the European Union (other than acts to which the first paragraph of Article 275 of the Treaty on the Functioning of the European Union applies);
> (c) acts adopted by the institutions of the European Communities in force immediately before the entry into force of the Lisbon Treaty; and
> (d) acts adopted by bodies competent under those treaties (other than acts to which the first paragraph of the said Article 275 applies)."

The supremacy of EU law was first recognised as part of the rule of law by Irish courts in *Pigs and Bacon Commission v McCarron* [1981] 1 I.R. 451. In *Campus Oil v Minister for Industry and Energy (No. 2)* [1983] I.R. 88, the Supreme Court held that EU law will always take precedence over Irish law, even provisions of the Constitution. In *Crotty v An Taoiseach* [1987] I.R. 713, the Supreme Court held that the ratification of the Single European Act by Ireland was not necessitated by membership of the European Communities and could therefore be subject to review by the courts. In *KD v DPP* [2016] IEHC 21, which dealt with whether or not the Victims' Rights Directive (2012/29/EU) had direct effect in Ireland, Humphries J. referred to the "clear" supremacy of EU law over Irish law. In *O'Shea v Westwood* [2015] IEHC 24, it was referred to as "well established". For further discussion of supremacy in Irish law, see *O'Sullivan v Sea Fisheries Protection Agency* [2016] IEHC 77 or *EPA v Harte Peat* [2014] IEHC 308.

The Preliminary Reference Mechanism

6

Introduction

A preliminary reference (also known as a reference for a preliminary ruling) is a procedure where a ruling is given by the Court of Justice on the interpretation of EU law, made at the request of a court of a Member State. This instrument is another of the mechanisms used to ensure that EU law is interpreted and applied uniformly throughout the Member States. It is similar to the case stated procedure in Irish law as it is a lower court asking a superior court for advice on interpreting the law. The preliminary reference was one of the primary engines behind the development of EU law. Many, if not most, of the most important CJEU decisions were originally preliminary references: *Van Gend En Loos* (C-26/62), *Costa v Enel* (C-6/64), *Van Duyn v The Home Office* (C-41/74), *Von Colson* (C-14/83), *Francovitch and Bonifaci v Italy* (C-6/90; C-9/90), *Brasserie du Pechuer and Factortame* (C-46/93; C-48/93), *Cassis de Dijon* (C-120/78), *Defrenne v Sabena* (C-43/75), *Reyners v Belgium* (C-2/74), *Bosman* (C-415/93), *Simmenthal* (C-106/77) and many, many more.

Reference for a Preliminary Ruling

Preliminary references are governed by art.267 TFEU. It states:

> "The Court of Justice of the European Union shall have jurisdiction to give preliminary rulings concerning:
> (a) the interpretation of the Treaties;
> (b) the validity and interpretation of acts of the institutions, bodies, offices or agencies of the Union;
> Where such a question is raised before any court or tribunal of a Member State, that court or tribunal may, if it considers that a decision on the question is necessary to enable it to give judgment, request the Court to give a ruling thereon.

Where any such question is raised in a case pending before a court or tribunal of a Member State against whose decisions there is no judicial remedy under national law, that court or tribunal shall bring the matter before the Court.

If such a question is raised in a case pending before a court or tribunal of a Member State with regard to a person in custody, the Court of Justice of the European Union shall act with the minimum of delay."

These court procedures are called a reference for a preliminary ruling because the national court will refer the matter to the CJEU for it to answer questions about the interpretation or validity of EU law. Until these questions have been answered, the national court will put a stay on its own proceedings (meaning to pause them). They are preliminary in that they are decided before the case is ultimately decided. The national court still decides the case, the Court of Justice only decides on the interpretation of EU law. Preliminary rulings are restricted to decisions solely on:

(a) the interpretation of the Treaties; and
(b) the validity and interpretation of acts of the institutions, bodies, offices or agencies of the Union.

A preliminary ruling can be sought at any point during a case; however, in *Irish Creamery Milk Suppliers Association v Ireland* (C-36/80), it was held that it is better to wait until the questions of national law and the facts of the case have been decided so that the Court of Justice can check if EU law applies. The Court has also recommended that the reference should be made only after both sides have been heard. In *Foglia v Novello (No. 2)* (C-244/80), the Court held it will not answer a preliminary reference where the questions are hypothetical or where there is not a genuine dispute. The CJEU can only give rulings on matters which are pending before the national courts; in *Fratelli Pardini* (C-338/85), it held it could not rule where the case had finished before the national court. The Court also does not have jurisdiction to answer a preliminary reference about national legislation which falls outside of EU law; this was decided in *Kremzow v Austria* (C-299/95), which was about a judge convicted of murder.

Court or Tribunal

The meaning of "court or tribunal of a Member State" is a matter of EU law and is not determined by the laws of the Member States. It does not matter whether or not the body calls itself a court or tribunal. Article 267 does not define "court or tribunal". In *Doris Saltzmann* (C-178/99), a number of factors were considered when deciding whether or not a body is a "court or tribunal", including whether:

- it is established by law;
- it is permanent;
- its jurisdiction is compulsory;
- it has inter partes procedure;
- it is independent; and
- it applies rules of law.

However, these are not absolute. In *Broekmeulen v Huisarts Registratie Commissie* (C-248/80), the applicant was a Dutchman registered as a doctor in Belgium, he wanted to register as a doctor in Holland and was refused. The CJEU ruled that the Dutch Appeals Committee for General Medicine was a "court or tribunal" within the meaning of the Treaty and could therefore make a reference for a preliminary ruling, even though that society was a private association and was not regarded as a court in Dutch law. In *Nederlandse Spoorwegen* (C-36/73), a state body was found to be covered; while in theory its decisions were only advisory, in practice it functioned as the Supreme Administrative Court of the Netherlands. This shows that the CJEU will look to the reality rather than to the theory behind the courts. In *Job Center Coop* (C-111/94), the Court held that a national court is not acting as a court or tribunal when it is carrying out administrative functions.

"Institutes, bodies, offices or agencies" refers to the seven EU institutions. Bodies which have been found not to be covered are those which are created by the law of Member States including government departments, public corporations and local government authorities, even where they are acting under EU law.

Obligation to Refer

Any court can make a request for a preliminary reference, although some courts are obliged to make preliminary references if requested. Under art.267(3) TFEU, a court is under the obligation to refer where a question is raised in a case pending before a court or tribunal of a Member State, against whose decisions there is no judicial remedy in domestic law, and the answer is necessary for the court to reach a decision. In Ireland, this means the Supreme Court. In *Foto Frost* (C-314/85), it was held that national courts do not have authority to find EU law invalid; instead, they are obliged to refer to the CJEU even where they are not a final court of appeal. There the national court was examining a Directive in the light of a Regulation. The reason the court cannot find the act invalid is to ensure EU law is the same in all Member States. In *Cartesio* (C-210/06), it was held that if you can appeal but only on a point of law rather than on the facts, then there is an appeal and, therefore, there is no obligation to refer. In *Lyckeskog* (C-99/00), it was held that where permission must be given for an appeal by the Supreme Court, there is no obligation to refer.

Exceptions to Obligation to Refer

There are a number of exceptions to the obligation to refer: *acte éclairé*, *acte clair* and where no question of EU law arises.

Acte éclairé

A court is not under an obligation to refer if the question that has arisen has already been answered in an earlier judgment of the Court of Justice. This can be seen as being like a system of precedent. In joined cases *Da Costa en Schaake* (C-28–30/62), the facts of the case and questions of law were identical to those in *Van Gen den Loos*. This previous ruling removed the national court's obligation to refer. In *CILFIT* (C-283/81), it was held there is no obligation to refer on the same point of law even if the facts of the case are not identical.

Acte clair

A court is also not obliged to refer if the question has not yet been answered, but the answer to that question is obvious beyond all doubt. This doctrine comes from *CILFIT* where the court held they must

> "be convinced that that the matter is equally obvious to the courts of the other Member States and to the Court of Justice. Only if these conditions are satisfied may the national court or tribunal refrain from submitting the question of the Court of Justice and take upon itself responsibility for resolving it."

In coming to this conclusion the national court should bear in mind that:

- the interpretation of a provision of EU law involves a comparison of the different language versions of the provision concerned;
- terms and concepts in EU law do not necessarily have the same meaning as the laws of the various Member States; and

- every provision of EU law should be interpreted in the light of EU law as a whole, taking into consideration its objectives and its state of development at the moment of application of the provision in question.

No question of EU law arises

The Court in *CILFIT* also held that there is no obligation to refer if the national court or tribunal is of the opinion that no question of EU law arises.

Forming the Reference

The Court in *Commission v Ireland* (36/80) emphasised that it is for the national courts to decide at which stage in the proceedings they make a reference for a preliminary ruling. In *Holdijk* (C-141–143/81), the Court of Justice set out a number of guidelines surrounding the formulation of Article 267 references. The CJEU has also issued non-binding recommendations (2012/C 338/01) to national courts on the formulation of preliminary references.

The CJEU encourages the inclusion of relevant background information in the reference. This is to prevent abuse of process and to help it decide if it has jurisdiction. The reference should be self-explanatory and self-contained. The national court must explain why the reference is necessary, unless it is self-evident from the file. The general legal context must be defined to allow the CJEU to give a ruling which will help the national court. It makes things easier if the facts have been settled along with the matters of national law. The CJEU has held in *Telemarsicabrizzo* (C-320/90) that references are inadmissible where the background is not sufficiently factual. As the reference needs to be translated into all of the official languages of the European Union, it should be drafted in simple, clear language, avoiding unnecessary detail. The reference should contain a summary of the dispute and facts, the national law and a statement of the reasons why the court has made the preliminary reference.

When a national body refers a question to the CJEU, the research and documentation department of the Court carries out a check to see if the referring body is a court or tribunal of a Member State; whether the subject matter falls within the jurisdiction of the CJEU; whether the dispute is genuine; and whether the factual and legal context is clearly set out.

Other Points

A reference for a preliminary ruling is not an appeal—it is a reference by a national court to the CJEU from one judge to another. There are two major differences here. The first difference is that an appeal is initiated by parties to the case who are unhappy with the outcome or a judge's decision; they will decide to bring an appeal and will take the necessary procedural steps to do so themselves. A court that is being appealed has no say in the matter. In a reference for a preliminary ruling, it is up to the judge to make the reference, not the parties, and it is up to the judge to initiate things. The second difference between an appeal and a preliminary reference is that an appeal court decides the case only and can substitute its own decision with that of the lower court. In a preliminary reference, the court has the facts already decided and it is for it to decide on the law on those facts. It does not overrule the decisions of the national courts and cannot apply its interpretation of the law to the facts.

In Irish law there is no appeal from a refusal to make a reference for a preliminary ruling (*Campus Oil v Minister for Industry and Energy (No. 2)* [1983] I.R. 88).

Procedure

Once the reference is before the CJEU, the parties, along with Member States and the Commission, can make oral and written submissions. The Council can also do so if the reference is about one of the acts. The main issue is the reference and parties are limited to making suggestions to the Court as to how it should be interpreted. The Court cannot make rulings as to the facts of the case, although they can decide as a matter of fact if an EU act is valid. If it is doing this, it will use the normal court procedure and can hear witnesses.

The time limits for a reference are shorter when the question concerns a person in custody as this is more urgent. Here there may be restrictions on the right to submit statements or written observations. In very urgent cases, the written stage of the procedure may be entirely excluded. Under the rules of procedure, there is a mechanism for expedited and urgent procedures; these are used, for example, in cases involving the custody of children. Preliminary reference cases take an average of 15 months, so the need for faster procedure in some cases is clear.

When deciding the reference, the court will pass judgment, setting out the facts and background of the case, discussing the questions posed and giving the reasons for the rulings on the various issues posed. Once the preliminary reference has been answered by the CJEU, it will send the case back to the national court which made the reference which will apply the European law. A preliminary ruling is binding not only on the court which made the reference but also on the courts of all Member States. In *International Chemical Corporation* (66/80), the CJEU held that a judgment declaring an EU measure illegal bound all courts and authorities in the EU. It is only binding as to what the law of the European Union is, the national court may still decide the case on other grounds. The national court is not bound to apply the law, but if it does apply it, it is bound by the ruling in the preliminary ruling. While the CJEU is limited to deciding the law in question, the CJEU's ruling frequently leaves little room for the national court to rule other than in a specific way.

Cases Stated and Preliminary Ruling Procedure

In Irish law, there is a legal procedure known as a case stated. A case stated is a question of law from a lower court that can be answered by higher court with a "yes" or "no". If during the hearing, a point of law arises which requires to be ruled on, the parties may agree to refer the issue of law to the higher court for an answer. The judge will lay out the facts as agreed and give the question of law, which has been prepared by the parties and signed off by the parties. The question will usually be phrased along the lines of: "Am I correct in deciding X?".

This is very similar to preliminary rulings. One major difference between a case stated and a preliminary reference is that you can appeal by way of case stated. A preliminary reference is not an appeal. There are two types of cases stated: a consultative case stated and an appeal by way of case stated. Of these, a consultative case stated is more like the preliminary ruling procedure. A consultative case stated is made at the discretion of a judge before he or she determines the case before the court. An appeal by way of case stated is made at the request of a party to the proceedings to the judge after the conclusion of a case.

A case stated from the District Court will go to the High Court and a case stated from the Circuit Court will go to the Court of Appeal.

7 Judicial Review of European Union Law

INTRODUCTION

Judicial review of EU law is governed by arts 263–266 TFEU and is called an annulment action. This is a legal procedure where the Court of Justice reviews the legality of acts of the European institutions, bodies, offices or organisations and will annul those acts which are against EU law. These actions give citizens protection against the actions of the institutions and bodies of the European Union. Unlike other, more settled, areas of European law, this is still somewhat in flux. There are four things that need to be satisfied before an act can be successfully challenged. First, the relevant body being challenged must be one which can be judicially reviewed. Secondly, the act must be of a kind which is open to challenge. Thirdly, the institution or person taking the challenge must have locus standi or standing to take the case. Finally, the case must be taken within the specified time limits. In looking at this topic we will look at:

1. Reviewable Acts—what cases can be judicially reviewed;
2. Standing and privileged applicants—who can take a case and why; and
3. Grounds for and effects of annulment—when and why a case can be taken and what will happen if it succeeds.

ANNULMENT ACTIONS

Article 263 TFEU states:

> "The Court of Justice of the European Union shall review the legality of legislative acts, of acts of the Council, of the Commission and of the European Central Bank, other than recommendations and opinions, and of acts of the European Parliament and of the European Council intended to produce legal effects vis-à-vis third parties. It shall also review the legality of acts of bodies, offices or agencies of the Union intended to produce legal effects vis-à-vis third parties.

It shall for this purpose have jurisdiction in actions brought by a Member State, the European Parliament, the Council or the Commission on grounds of lack of competence, infringement of an essential procedural requirement, infringement of the Treaties or of any rule of law relating to their application, or misuse of powers.

The Court shall have jurisdiction under the same conditions in actions brought by the Court of Auditors, by the European Central Bank and by the Committee of the Regions for the purpose of protecting their prerogatives.

Any natural or legal person may, under the conditions laid down in the first and second paragraphs, institute proceedings against an act addressed to that person or which is of direct and individual concern to them, and against a regulatory act which is of direct concern to them and does not entail implementing measures.

Acts setting up bodies, offices and agencies of the Union may lay down specific conditions and arrangements concerning actions brought by natural or legal persons against acts of these bodies, offices or agencies intended to produce legal effects in relation to them.

The proceedings provided for in this Article shall be instituted within two months of the publication of the measure, or of its notification to the plaintiff, or, in the absence thereof, of the day on which it came to the knowledge of the latter, as the case may be."

Article 264 states:

"If the action is well founded, the Court of Justice of the European Union shall declare the act concerned to be void.

However, the Court shall, if it considers this necessary, state which of the effects of the act which it has declared void shall be considered as definitive."

Article 265 states:

"Should the European Parliament, the European Council, the Council, the Commission or the European Central Bank, in infringement of the Treaties, fail to act, the Member States and the other institutions of the Union may bring an action before the Court of Justice of the European Union to have the infringement established. This Article shall apply, under the same conditions, to bodies, offices and agencies of the Union which fail to act.

The action shall be admissible only if the institution, body, office or agency concerned has first been called upon to act. If, within two months of being so called upon, the institution, body, office or agency concerned has not defined its position, the action may be brought within a further period of two months.

Any natural or legal person may, under the conditions laid down in the preceding paragraphs, complain to the Court that an institution, body, office or agency of the Union has failed to address to that person any act other than a recommendation or an opinion."

Article 266 states:

"The institution whose act has been declared void or whose failure to act has been declared contrary to the Treaties shall be required to take the necessary measures to comply with the judgment of the Court of Justice of the European Union.

This obligation shall not affect any obligation which may result from the application of the second paragraph of Article 340."

Reviewable Acts

Article 263(1) allows the court to review the legality of acts, taken by the Council, the Commission, the European Central Bank, the European Parliament and the European Council. It covers Regulations, Decisions and Directives but does not cover recommendations and opinions as they are not legally binding. From art.263 we can see that legislative acts other than recommendations and opinions can be reviewed along with acts intended to produce legal effects against third parties.

The test whether an act can be reviewed looks at the legal effect of the act and not how it appears. If an act does not change anyone's legal position, but only confirms a previous act, it has no legal effect and therefore is not reviewable (*SNUPAT v High Commission* (C-59/69)). In *Commission v Council* (22/70) (the ERTA case), the Court held that an act is reviewable if it is legally binding, even if does not fall into any of the categories of art.288. In *IBM v Commission* (C-60/81), the computer giant IBM sought to annul a letter informing it that the Commission had begun competition law proceedings against it. The Commission claimed that the letter was not an act which could be reviewed. The Court of Justice held that you must look to the substance of the acts to see whether they were acts for the purpose of art.263. Any measure which has a binding legal effect on a party or which could affect their legal interests by bringing about a change in their position can be reviewed under art.263. The form that the acts take is irrelevant. Where the acts are part of a multi-stage procedure, they can only be reviewed if they were the final stage. Here the statement of objections did not alter IBM's position and it lost its application.

Failure to Act

Annulment actions can also be taken for failure to act under art.265. These can be taken against the European Parliament, the European Council, the Council of the European Union, the European Commission and the European Central Bank. The biggest difference between this and an Article 263 action is that you must first put the institution on notice to fulfil its duty before you can take this action. Any subsequent annulment proceedings are defined by the terms of this request. The EU institution's reply is called "a definition of position". The institution has two months within which to comply with this notice and then there are a further two months within which the case can be taken. The other main difference between this and an Article 263 action is that the latter can be taken for four grounds, whereas an Article 265 action can only be taken for one.

The order sought in an action taken by the institutions against another institution is a declaration that the body concerned has infringed the Treaty by neglecting to take a decision required of it. Where the action is brought by an individual, it is for a declaration that the institution has infringed the Treaty by neglecting to address an individual decision to it. The judgment simply finds that the neglect was unlawful. The Court of Justice/General Court has no jurisdiction to order that a decision be taken. The party against whom the judgment is given is merely required to take measures to comply with the judgment.

Standing and Privileged Applicants

If somebody wants to take a case, they must have legal standing or locus standi to do so. If someone does not have sufficient standing, they are not entitled to take the case, even if it would otherwise succeed. Lack of standing means that even if a measure was wrong and would be struck down, you cannot take a case if it does not affect you. The purpose of the locus standi rule, according to O'Higgins C.J. in the Irish case of *Cahill v Sutton* [1980] 1 I.R. 269, is to stop the courts from becoming "the happy hunting ground of the busybody and the crank".

In an EU judicial review case, there are three main types of applicant that can take a case. There are privileged applicants, quasi-privileged applicants and non-privileged applicants.

Privileged applicants

Article 263 sets out several categories of plaintiff. The first are preferential plaintiffs or privileged plaintiffs. These are the Member States, the European Commission, the European Parliament and the European Council. These applicants are "preferential", meaning that they can take an annulment action without having to prove standing or show that they are in any way affected by the case.

EU law does not oblige a Member State to take an action in order to benefit one of its citizens, but it does not prevent a Member State from taking such an action (*Netherlands v Ten Kate Holding* (C-511/03)).

Quasi-privileged applicants

Certain applicants can take certain specific actions; they are known as quasi-privileged applicants. The Court of Auditors, the European Central Bank and the Committee of the Regions may bring actions against acts which they believe undermine their prerogatives. Their prerogatives are laid out in the TFEU; for example, art.287 lays out the prerogatives of the Court of Auditors. Quasi-privileged applicants are required to prove that they are protecting their prerogatives when they are taking an annulment action. National parliaments and the Committee of the Regions may bring annulment actions against acts which, in their view, are contrary to the principle of subsidiarity.

Non-privileged applicants

Natural and legal persons may also take an annulment action. They are the category of non-preferential or non-privileged applicants. Article 263(4) TFEU states:

> "Any natural or legal person may ... institute proceedings against an act addressed to that person or which is of direct and individual concern to them, and *against a regulatory act which is of direct concern to them and does not entail implementing measures*" (emphasis added).

Natural and legal persons must show an interest in taking action in order to request the annulment of a European act. This means that the contested act must be addressed to the applicant or must concern him or her directly and individually. In *Plaumann & Co v Commission* (C-25/62), being adversely affected by rising duties was not enough to show interest. In *Toepfer v Commission* (C-106–107/63), an applicant, an importer, was held to be individually concerned because the decision to refuse an import licence only applied to importers who applied on a particular day. Likewise, in *Bock v Commission* (C-62/70), the Court found the applicant to be individually concerned because:

> "A decision is of individual concern to a person when the factual situation created by the decision differentiates him from all other persons and distinguishes him individually just as in the case of the person addressed. A trader is therefore individually concerned by a decision authorizing a Member State to reject the application for an import license made by the said trader prior to the adoption of the decision if the State makes use of that authorization."

Cases taken by non-privileged applicants are heard before the General Court, whereas the cases taken by privileged and quasi-privileged applicants are heard by the Court of Justice. This is presumably to filter out the busybodies and cranks. It is clear that many cases taken by individuals are filtered out. Since the Court interpreted the standing conditions narrowly, in particular as it concerned the requirement of individual concern, it was extremely difficult for private persons to succeed in bringing an action for annulment. This is confirmed by statistical data: the number of annulment actions deemed inadmissible during the years of 2001–2005 by the General Court (58.6 per cent) was more than five times higher than that of the Court of Justice (10.7 per cent).

Since the drafting of the unratified Treaty establishing a Constitution for Europe, the exact meaning of the wording "regulatory act" under art.263(4) has been the subject of debate. This is mainly because neither that Treaty, nor the Lisbon Treaty, has a definition of a "regulatory act" and this phrase is not used in any other articles of the Treaties. The matter was dealt with in the case of *Inuit Tapiriit Kanatami v European Parliament* (T-526/10).

Inuit

Inuit was brought by parties involved in the trade of seal products, in particular, a non-profit Canadian organisation representing Inuit people. They sought the annulment of a Regulation which limited the circumstances in which seal products could be marketed. The General Court noted that "regulatory act" is not defined within the TFEU and rejected the idea of limiting regulatory acts to delegated acts. The Court held that the term "regulatory act" should be defined as "an act of general application which is not a legislative act".

The Court went on to reject the submissions of the parties for a wider definition of "regulatory act" based on the right to effective judicial protection in art.47 of the EU Charter. As the Regulation in question was adopted under what is now the ordinary legislative procedure, it was classified as a legislative act. The applicants had to establish both direct and individual concern. As all of the applicants failed to satisfy this test, the action was inadmissible.

The General Court subsequently considered the same issue in *Microban International v European Commission* (T-262/10). The applicant here produced and marketed Triclosan, a material used in food packaging. They were challenging a European Commission Decision which prohibited the use of Triclosan in products which come into contact with food. The Court confirmed the definition given in *Inuit*. Since the regulatory act here did not entail implementing measures, the applicants did not have to show they were individually concerned and the action was admitted and the act was annulled.

Time Limits

Applicants have a period of two months to bring an action for annulment under art.263. This period begins either from the date of publication of the measure, the date of its notification to the applicant, or of the day on which it came to the knowledge of the latter. In article 265 cases, applicants must first call upon the institution to act. The institution has two months to comply with this and the applicant then has a further two months within which to take the case. The Treaties do not specify any time limits within which the procedure for failure to act should be taken, the Court has said it should be within a reasonable time (*Netherlands v Commission* (59/70)). It is possible to object to the illegality of an act in a court case other than a case founded on annulment proceedings, even if it is outside the time limits for judicial review, under art.277 TFEU.

Acts Which Can be Annulled

The following acts can be annulled.

Regulations

Regulations are directly applicable EU legal acts, which means that they do not require national implementing measures. If someone wants to challenge a regulation, not only is it possible for them to seek an annulment action, this is the only way they can.

Directives

A Directive is defined as a legal act, binding as to the result to be achieved upon each Member State to which it is addressed, but leaving to the national authorities the choice of form and methods. As a result, Directives always require national implementing measures, so proving direct and individual concern can be very difficult. In joined cases *Salamander* (T-172/98, T-175–177/98), the Court stated that the Directive cannot of itself impose obligations on the applicants as such obligation can arise only from the transposition measures adopted by the Member States, and therefore does not concern the applicants directly.

On the other hand, since Directives are implemented in national laws, the national implementing measures may be subjected to judicial review procedures in national courts, which may refer to the European courts for a preliminary ruling.

Decisions

The addressee of the Decision has an automatic right to challenge it before the Court. For example, Decisions of the European Commission for infringement of competition law are commonly challenged by their addressees and standing is granted without any discussions. Where a Decision is addressed to someone else, it can only be challenged if an applicant is directly and individually concerned by it.

Recommendations and Opinions

As we have already seen, Recommendations and Opinions are not legally binding; this means that they do not have legal effect and therefore are not reviewable.

Grounds for Annulment

Once an Article 263 action has been referred to the Court of Justice, it will assess whether the act complies with EU law. The Court can annul the act based on the following four grounds:

- lack of competence;
- infringement of an essential procedural requirement;
- infringement of the Treaties or of any rule of law relating to their application; and
- misuse of powers.

Lack of competence

One of the fundamental principles of judicial review, both in Irish and EU law, is that institutions cannot act beyond their powers. If they do, they will be said to have acted ultra vires. EU institutions have to act within the powers given to them by the Treaties or legal acts based on the Treaties. These powers are known as competences. If they go beyond them, any ultra vires act will be declared void for lack of competence. Article 5 TEU provides:

> "1. The limits of Union competences are governed by the principle of conferral. The use of Union competences is governed by the principles of subsidiarity and proportionality.
>
> 2. Under the principle of conferral, the Union shall act only within the limits of the competences conferred upon it by the Member States in the Treaties to attain the objectives set out therein. Competences not conferred upon the Union in the Treaties remain with the Member States."

In *Germany v Commission* (C-282–287/85), five Member States sought to annul a Decision of the European Commission dealing with immigration from non-Member States on the grounds that the Commission lacked competence. The Decision was found to be void in part. The Commission had limited power to make legally binding decisions but had not expressed the treaty article giving it the power to make this Decision. The legal basis only covered part of the subject matter of the Decision and, therefore, it was declared void in part. In *Boyle v Commission* (T-218–240/03), a group of Irish fishermen successfully challenged a European Commission Decision which introduced new criteria for funding as the original legislation did not give the Commission power to do this.

Infringement of an essential procedural requirement

Where an essential procedural requirement has been infringed, the action will be annulled. Just because a procedural requirement has been infringed does not mean an action will be annulled. Non-essential breaches of procedure will not result in annulment. Examples of non-essential breaches include a decision containing an error as to the date on which it had been adopted, a verbal rather than written decision, and a Council Directive in which no reference had been made to the proposal of the Commission.

Examples of infringements of essential procedural requirements include infringements of the right to be heard, breaches of the duty to give reasons, and cases where the duties of consultation and participation are violated. In *Roquette Frères v Council* (C-138/79), an essential procedural requirement was infringed where the Council of the European Communities was deemed to have interfered with the consultation procedure by adopting a measure without waiting for the Parliament's opinion; this was an infringement. In *Transocean*

Marine Paint v Commission (C-17/74), a Decision was in breach of the duty to provide reasons and in *Germany v Commission* (C-24/62), a Regulation was made on an incorrect legal basis and was in breach of the obligation to state reasons. In a case where it is claimed the European Commission violated the right to be heard, the claimant does not have to show that the Commission's decision would have been different, but simply that the possibility cannot be ruled out since it would have been better placed to defend itself if it had had a chance to be heard (*Yongjian Housewears* (C-141/08)).

Infringement of the Treaties or of any rule of law relating to their application

This ground provided the foundation for the development of the principles of judicial review and, as a result, there is a lot of overlap between this grounds and the two previous grounds. Infringement of the treaty means any article of any of the Treaties. Unfortunately, there is no guidance on what any rule relating to their application means. It is probably the case that it means Regulations, Directives, etc. passed pursuant to the Treaties, but this is yet to be clarified.

Misuse of powers

In *Gutmann v Commission* (C-18 and 35/65), the CJEU stated that: "A decision may amount to an abuse of powers if it appears, on the basis of objective relevant and consistent facts, to have been taken for purposes other than those stated." The applicant was a Euratom official transferred on the basis of a provision which authorised the transfer of individuals "[i]n the interests of the service". The Court of Justice held that the real reason for his transfer was for disciplinary reasons. The decision was therefore annulled for misuse of powers. In *UK v Council of the EU* (C-84/94), the Court of Justice referred to a decision taken with "[t]he exclusive or main purpose of achieving an end other than that stated or evading a procedure specifically prescribed by the Treaty for dealing with the circumstances of the case."

In *Giuffrida v Council* (C-105/75), the case concerned a job application; the applicant had applied for a job in a Directorate-General for Regional Policy. The specified requirements in the job advertisement were designed so that only one specific person could get the job. This appointment to an administrative position was, in fact, purely to avoid internal problems. These unusual requirements made it impossible for the applicant to be qualified for the job. It was held to be a misuse of powers and was struck down.

Effects of Annulment

If the action is successful, the court may annul the act in its entirety or certain provisions only. The annulled act or provisions will no longer have legal effect. The institution, body, office or organisation which adopted the act is required to fill the resulting legal void in accordance with the judgment delivered by the court. When the case is before the court, the effect of the challenged law is not suspended automatically (art.278 TFEU), although it can be and the court can prescribe any interim measures which are necessary.

The question as to what will happen to national legislation that was enacted to transpose an invalid directive has yet to be answered. An example of a recently annulled Directive was the Data Retention Directive (Directive 2006/24/EC). The CJEU held that this should be annulled because it was not compatible with EU law, although it may interfere with basic fundamental rights such as privacy. However, the CJEU also found that the set of obligations laid down in this Directive was disproportionate because "the wide ranging and particularly serious interference of the directive with the fundamental rights at issue is not sufficiently circumscribed to ensure that that interference is actually limited to what is strictly necessary."

Irish Judicial Review

Judicial review in Ireland is a type of court proceeding where a judge of the High Court reviews the lawfulness of a decision or an action of the inferior courts, tribunals and a wide variety of other administrators. Denham J. noted in *Dekra Éireann Teo. v Minister for the Environment* [2003] 2 I.R. 270 that: "In the course of the last two decades, throughout the common law world, there has been an explosion in litigation by way of judicial review". Judicial review is one of the most common forms of cases taken in Ireland, with around one third of cases brought in the High Court being judicial review.

Irish judicial review is like EU judicial review in many ways. The time limits are much shorter than in other areas of law, three months in Irish law and two months in EU law. The remedies are also very similar; the main remedy most often sought is certiorari, which is a quashing order similar to that remedy provided by art.263. The second most commonly sought remedy is mandamus, which is an order compelling someone to act. This is similar to that remedy provided by art.265, although, as the Irish courts can compel parties to act, mandamus is clearly a stronger remedy than art.265. The grounds for and effects of Irish judicial review are very like those in EU law. For more information on Irish judicial review, please see M. Holmes, *Administrative Law Nutshell* (Dublin: Round Hall, 2014).

Enforcement of EU Law

8

Introduction

EU law must be enforced if it is to have any effect. This means that if it is breached there must be consequences. EU law is enforced in two ways. The first is in the courts of the Member States by individuals when their EU rights have been infringed. The second is in the CJEU against Member States who have infringed EU law. These cases are taken by the European Commission or by other Member States. This chapter will analyse both of these forms of enforcement in turn.

National Enforcement

Article 19 TEU states: "Member States shall provide remedies sufficient to ensure effective legal protection in the fields covered by Union law."

Article 47 of the Charter of Fundamental Rights and Freedoms states:

> "Everybody whose rights and freedoms guaranteed by the law of the union are violated has the right to an effective remedy before a tribunal in compliance with the conditions laid down in this Article."

National legal rules of procedure are the rules which cover the way in which cases are run before courts and tribunals. They include things like who can take a case, time limits within which cases must be taken, how cases should be brought, which remedies the courts can give, how compensation is awarded, what proofs are needed, how witnesses and evidence are dealt with, and what documents need to be filed. This principle of national regional autonomy is discussed below.

Remedies for Violation of European Law

Direct effect allows people to rely on their rights which have been created by EU law in a national court. It is all well and good saying this; however, if national courts cannot provide them with some kind of remedy for the breach of an EU right, there is no point in having it. As a general rule, EU law does not provide remedies for the infringement of the rights it gives (bar in specific, limited cases). This is because legal procedural rules were not within the competences of the Treaties. Instead, EU law is enforced in the courts of Member States according to national procedural rules and national remedies. As seen above, art.19 TEU requires Member States to provide legal remedies to ensure protection in the fields covered by European Union law.

It was clear from *Van Gend en Loos* (C-26/62) that citizens could rely on their national courts to remedy breaches of European rights. In *Simmenthal* (C-108/77), the Court held: "Every national court must, in a case within its jurisdiction, apply Community law in its entirety and protect rights which the latter confers on individuals." However, there was little discussion on how they would actually go about obtaining remedies. Without EU-wide remedies, the protection of EU rights could be weakened at national level. National legal procedural rules could make it difficult to access a remedy and any remedies awarded might not be enough to compensate for any loss suffered. This poses a serious risk of undermining EU rights.

The doctrines of direct effect and supremacy have made the national courts the primary venue for legal proceedings regarding a Member State's compliance with EU law. As can be seen from the decision in *Marleasing SA* (C-106/89), direct effect does not require the European Commission to bring an action against the State. The national courts are most likely to be the places where the consequences of breaching EU law are determined. As a result, the response of these courts to domestic breaches of EU law will decide how effective EU law is in practise. The Court of Justice ensures the effectiveness of national enforcement of EU law by laying down standards as to the remedies these national courts must provide.

Originally the CJEU said there was no requirement for Member States to create new remedies for EU law. In *Norddeutsches Vieh- und Fleischkontor GMBH* (C-39/70), the Court held:

> "Where national authorities are responsible for implementing a Community regulation it must be recognised that in principle this implementation takes place with due respect for the forms and procedures of national law."

In *Comet* (C-45/76), the Court confirmed this national remedial autonomy principle. The national remedial autonomy principle is the principle which says that, in the absence of a specific EU remedy to go with an EU right, it is up to legal systems of the Member States to set out rules controlling court proceedings enforcing EU rights. In *Rewe Handelsgescellshaft Nord* (C-158/80), the Court held: "It was not intended to create new remedies in the national courts to ensure the observance of Community law other than those already set down in national law." This approach subsequently changed. In *Heylens* (C-222/86), the Court stated:

> "Since free access to employment is a fundamental right which the Treaty confers individually on each migrant worker in the Community, the existence of a remedy of a judicial nature against any decision of a national authority refusing the benefit of that right is essential in order to secure for the individual effective protection for his right."

In *Francovich and Bonifaci v Italy* (C-6/90), Italy was required to introduce the remedy of damages. In *Marshall v Southampton and South West Hampshire Area Health Authority (Teaching) (No. 2)* (C-271/91), it was held that certain restrictions on compensation could not apply where the claim was based on EU law.

There are now two main principles governing remedies for breaches of EU law in national courts. They are:

1. Equivalence
2. Effectiveness

In *Rewe*, the Court suggested the principle of effectiveness requires that it must not be "excessively difficult or impossible for an individual to exercise his right to obtain a remedy" and that national authorities must secure effective remedies to protect EU rights. The principal of equivalence dictates that as long as national law provided a remedy for a breach of EU law which is similar to that which it provides for a breach of a similar national rule, that remedy would be lawful under EU law.

In *Grundig Italiana v Ministero delle Finanze* (C-255/00), it was held that

> "it is for the domestic legal system of each Member State to designate the courts and tribunals having jurisdiction and to lay down the detailed procedural rules governing actions for safeguarding rights which individuals derive from Community law, provided, first, that such rules are not less favourable than those governing similar domestic actions (principle of equivalence) and, secondly, that they do not render virtually impossible or excessively difficult the exercise of rights conferred by Community law (principle of effectiveness)."

EQUIVALENCE

The principle of equivalence makes sure that EU rights receive the same protection as domestic ones. Equivalence is also known as non-discrimination.

It means that the remedies and types of legal action available in national law must also be available to enforce EU law. Remedies for breaches of EU law cannot be less favourable than remedies for breaches of national law. Like cases must be treated alike; if national law guarantees a certain level of protection to domestic rights, EU rights should get the same level of protection as well. When national courts are applying EU law, they must act as if they are applying national law. This doctrine treats EU law as if it were national law; the same remedies and types of legal action must be available for breaches of both. In *Levezz v Jennings* (C-326), the CJEU held:

> "The principle of equivalence requires that the rule at issue be applied without distinction, whether the infringement alleged is of Community law or national law, where the *purpose and cause of action* are similar …
>
> In order to determine whether the principle of equivalence has been complied with in the present case, the national court — which alone has direct knowledge of the procedural rules governing actions in the field of employment law — must consider both *the purpose and the essential characteristics* of allegedly similar domestic actions" (emphasis added).

In joined cases i-21 *Germany GmbH and Arcor v Germany* (C-392/04 and 422/04), the Court held:

> "In relation to the principle of equivalence, this requires that all the rules applicable to appeals, including the prescribed time-limits, apply without distinction to appeals on the ground of infringement of Community law and to appeals on the ground of disregard of national law … Where, pursuant to rules of national law, the authorities are required to withdraw an administrative decision which has become final if that decision is manifestly incompatible with domestic law, that same obligation must exist if the decision is manifestly incompatible with Community law."

Effectiveness

Effectiveness means that national legal rules and procedures should not make the exercise of EU rights impossible in practice. Article 19 TEU says "Member States shall provide remedies sufficient to ensure *effective* legal protection in the fields covered by Union law" (emphasis added). Article 47 of the Charter of Fundamental Rights states:

"Everyone whose rights and freedoms guaranteed by the law of the Union are violated has the right to an *effective* remedy before a tribunal in compliance with the conditions laid down in this Article" (emphasis added).

The doctrine of effectiveness developed through the case law. In *Von Colson* (C-14/83), German women had been denied jobs in the German Prison Service, contrary to the Equal Treatment Directive 2006/54/EC. The only remedy they received was compensation for their travel expenses. The CJEU held that the Directive did not require a specific form of sanction for unlawful discrimination but that it did require that the sanction guarantee a "real and effective" remedy. Specifically, the Directive

> "leaves the Member State free to choose between the different solutions suitable for achieving its objective, it nevertheless requires that if a Member State chooses to penalise breaches of that prohibition by the award of compensation, then in order to ensure that it is effective and that it has a deterrent effect, that compensation must in any event be adequate in relation to the damage sustained and must therefore amount to more than purely nominal compensation".

This means it must be effective. In *Dekker* (C-177/99), the Court condemned national procedural restrictions which "weakened considerably" the effectiveness of the right to equal treatment. In *Cotter and McDermott v Minister for Social Welfare* (C-377/89), it was held that allowing the Minister for Social Welfare to rely on the doctrine of unjust enrichment would allow the State to use its own unlawful behaviour to undermine the effectiveness of a directive.

It then appeared in subsequent cases that a more restrictive approach was being taken as regards the principle of effectiveness. In *Stenhorst-Neerings* (C-338/91), the CJEU found that a national statute of limitations was not an absolute bar to taking a case and, therefore, did not undermine effectiveness. In *Draehmpaelh* (C-180/95), it was held that a cap on damages could be permissible. However, the CJEU has not entirely sought to restrict effectiveness; in *Manfredi* (C-295–298/04), it held that in competition case law that it must be possible to be compensated for actual loss *and* potential loss.

In *Unibet (London)* (C-432/05), the Swedish Supreme Court referred a question asking if the doctrine of effectiveness and EU law obliged Member States to provide a type of legal action which would declare a national law to be incompatible with EU Law. The CJEU confirmed that effectiveness is a general principle of EU law stemming from the constitutional tradition of Member States and also from arts 6 and 13 of the ECHR. It held that effectiveness does not require that such an action be provided unless

> "it were apparent from the overall scheme of the national legal system in question that no legal remedy existed which made it possible to ensure, even indirectly, respect for an individual's rights under Community law."

In *Mono Car Styling* (C-12/08), it was held that

> "whilst it is, in principle, for national law to determine an individual's standing and legal interest in bringing proceedings, Community law nevertheless requires, in addition to observance of the principles of equivalence and effectiveness, that the national legislation does not undermine the right to effective judicial protection."

The biggest change introduced by the doctrine of effectiveness was in *Francovich*, which introduced the remedy for state liability in tort when a Member State failed in its obligations in relation to directives. For further information on this, see the section on State Liability in Ch.4—Direct Effect, Indirect Effect and State Liability.

EQUIVALENCE AND EFFECTIVENESS IN IRISH LAW

The leading Irish judgment here is that of Fennelly J. in *TD v Minister for Justice* [2014] 4 I.R. 277. In this case, South African nationals were judicially reviewing a refusal to grant refugee status and a deportation order. They claimed they were relying on rights conferred by a European directive that had not yet been properly transposed into Irish law and that, therefore, the State could not rely on the two-week time limit imposed by the Illegal Immigrants (Trafficking) Act 2000. Fennelly J. noted:

> "The principles of effectiveness and equivalence being rules designed to protect the rights of individuals who pursue claims based on EU law in the national court will necessarily, as the occasion arises, impose on the national court the obligation to set aside any conflicting rules of national law."

Fennelly J. gives a detailed analysis of the European case law before going on to hold:

> "The court should look at the substance of the rule whose compatibility is under scrutiny to see whether it is discriminatory. One looks at its essential scope and area of operation."

He then found that the relevant section did not breach the principles of equivalence or effectiveness.

Enforcement Actions against Member States

When a Member State infringes EU law, enforcement actions can be taken against it by the European Commission or by other Member States. These actions are governed by arts 258–260 TFEU. Article 258 governs actions taken by the Commission and art.259 governs actions taken by other Member States. In practice, for political reasons, it is usually the Commission that will seek to enforce the law. An example of where this type of procedure might be appropriate would be where a Member State refuses to transpose a directive. If a Member State fails to comply with a judgment given against it under these articles, the Commission has the possibility of a second court ruling ordering that State to pay a lump-sum fine or a penalty under art.260 TFEU. There are serious financial implications for a Member State which ignores a Court judgment. These actions are one of the three main kinds of actions the CJEU deals with, along with preliminary references and other direct actions.

Article 258 Enforcement Actions

The European Commission is the guardian of the Treaties; the Commissioners think in terms of the interests of the European Union rather than the interests of the Member States or the citizens. It is part of its job to ensure that EU law is complied with by taking Member States or other institutions to the Court of Justice in the event of a dispute, to ensure that EU law is enforced. The Commission learns of breaches of EU law from European Parliamentary questions, official journals, petitions, databases and the media. Citizens can take part by notifying the Commission that a Member State has failed to comply with European Law. The procedure which governs the Commission's enforcement of EU law can be found in art.258 TFEU. Article 258 has wide application and can be used for many different types of breaches of EU law, including acts or omissions which are breaches of obligations found in the Treaties, legislation or judgments. It states:

> "If the Commission considers that a Member State has failed to fulfil an obligation under the Treaties, it shall deliver a reasoned opinion on the matter after giving the State concerned the opportunity to submit its observations.
>
> If the State concerned does not comply with the opinion within the period laid down by the Commission, the latter may bring the matter before the Court of Justice of the European Union."

Opinions as we have previously seen are not legally binding, which is why they are not discussed in great levels of detail. They are issued by the institutions when giving an assessment of a situation or of developments in the Union or Member States. In some cases, such as here, they also prepare the way for subsequent legally binding acts, or are a prerequisite for the institution of proceedings before the Court of Justice.

PROCEEDINGS

There are two phases in Article 258 proceedings. The first is administrative, the second is judicial.

ADMINISTRATIVE PHASE

Treaty infringement proceedings are very serious matters. They are taken exclusively before the Court of Justice, never before the General Court. It is so serious that before the matter can go to court it must be preceded with a preliminary procedure within which the Member State is given an opportunity to submit its observations. The Member State will have the opportunity to explain itself and to come to an agreement with the European Commission. If this does not solve the problem, the Member State will be formally notified of the specific infringement alleged by the Commission in a letter of formal notice. They are normally given two months to reply, unless the matter is urgent, and the Commission then has a year to decide whether or not to take the case. The reason for these two months is to clarify which areas the Member State is being asked to provide observations on and to provide the Member State the information it needs in order to prepare its own defence. It is possible for the Member State to ask for an extension of time. After receiving the letter, there are three possibilities: (a) the Member State fixes any problems; (b) the matter is dropped because it becomes apparent that the Member State has not infringed EU law; or (c) it proceeds to the reasoned opinion stage.

If the Commission decides to proceed, it then gives a reasoned opinion which sets out the grounds of the alleged infringement. This marks the start of the period within which the Member State must comply if it wants to avoid the judicial stage. The reason for the opinion is to decide the subject matter of any action and to set out the Commission's position on the infringement. It requests that the Member State comply within a given time. The reasoned opinion is based on the letter of formal notice. It must give a detailed statement of the reasons the Commission thinks that the Member State has failed to fulfil its EU law obligations. Referral by the Commission to the Court of Justice opens the judicial phase.

Judicial phase

If the reasoned opinion is not complied with, it is then followed by the judicial phase in the Court of Justice. The only question in these proceedings is whether or not the Member State has breached its EU law obligations. The remedy provided here is a declaration, i.e. the Court of Justice says officially that the Member State has infringed EU law. It is then up to the Member State to comply with the judgment and end its infringement "as soon as possible". The judicial stage is made up of the referral to the Court, followed by the Court's ruling and, if this is not complied with, the financial penalty stage under art.260 of the Treaty on the Functioning of the European Union (TFEU).

Article 259 Enforcement Actions

The European Commission is not the only body which can take enforcement actions. Member States can take enforcement actions against each other under art.259 TFEU for failure to comply with their EU law obligations. Article 259 states:

> "A Member State which considers that another Member State has failed to fulfil an obligation under the Treaties may bring the matter before the Court of Justice of the European Union.
>
> Before a Member State brings an action against another Member State for an alleged infringement of an obligation under the Treaties, it shall bring the matter before the Commission.
>
> The Commission shall deliver a reasoned opinion after each of the States concerned has been given the opportunity to submit its own case and its observations on the other party's case both orally and in writing.
>
> If the Commission has not delivered an opinion within three months of the date on which the matter was brought before it, the absence of such opinion shall not prevent the matter from being brought before the Court."

This is rarely used as for political reasons as Member States prefer if enforcement actions are taken by the Commission as they do not want to be seen to be attacking each other. These actions tend to be used when a Member State wants to make a political point against another Member State.

Cases where this was used

France v UK (C-141/78)

France successfully argued that a British statutory instrument governing the size of prawn fishing nets was in breach of the Treaty. The UK had unilaterally adopted these measures to protect fishing stocks without consulting the Commission or other Member States and had done so without the approval of the Commission.

Belgium v Spain (C-388/95)

Belgium, Denmark, Holland, Finland and the UK took a case contending that a Spanish royal decree on the designations of wine was a quantitative restriction on imports. (For more on quantitative restriction, see Ch.11 on the free movement of goods.) Here it was held not to be quantitative restriction.

Citizens and enforcement

As seen above, citizens can have some role in enforcement actions; they can notify the European Commission of breaches of EU law obligations. However, they have no say in whether or not the Commission actually initiates enforcement actions against a Member State (*Star Fruit v Commission* (C-247/87)). In *Petrie v Commission* (T-191/99), it was held that as individuals are not parties to Article 258 proceedings, they cannot invoke the right to a fair hearing. In that case it was held that the citizens were not entitled to documents in an Article 258 enforcement case.

Article 260

What happens if it is found that a Member State has breached its obligations? As we have seen, there is a declaration by the court that the Member State has breached EU law. Member States are given a period time before having to comply or to negotiate a deal. Research shows that, in 2002, in just over 37 per cent of cases Member States failed to comply with judgments within 12 months. If a Member State fails to comply with a judgment, it is open to the European Commission to take further action against that Member State under art.260. It states:

"1. If the Court of Justice of the European Union finds that a Member State has failed to fulfil an obligation under the Treaties, the State shall be required to take the necessary measures to comply with the judgment of the Court.

2. If the Commission considers that the Member State concerned has not taken the necessary measures to comply with the judgment of the Court, it may bring the case before the Court after giving that State the opportunity to submit its observations. It shall specify the amount of the lump sum or penalty payment to be paid by the Member State concerned which it considers appropriate in the circumstances.

If the Court finds that the Member State concerned has not complied with its judgment it may impose a lump sum or penalty payment on it.

This procedure shall be without prejudice to Article 259.

3. When the Commission brings a case before the Court pursuant to Article 258 on the grounds that the Member State concerned has failed to fulfil its obligation to notify measures transposing a directive adopted under a legislative procedure, it may, when it deems appropriate, specify the amount of the lump sum or penalty payment to be paid by the Member State concerned which it considers appropriate in the circumstances.

If the Court finds that there is an infringement it may impose a lump sum or penalty payment on the Member State concerned not exceeding the amount specified by the Commission. The payment obligation shall take effect on the date set by the Court in its judgment."

If it is found that the Member State has not complied with the Article 258 or 259 judgment, the Court may impose a fine upon that Member State, either a lump sum or penalty payment or both. The European Commission issued guidelines on the application of the pre-Lisbon art.228 of the EC Treaty (which has now been replaced by art.260 TFEU), which indicate that it will ask for both penalties in such cases. These guidelines are now being revised to take into account the amendments introduced by art.260.

The fines mechanism was introduced by the Maastricht Treaty. In *Commission v Greece* (C-45/91), Greece was found to be in violation of its obligations regarding the dumping of toxic waste. Greece did nothing to remedy the breach as this was before Maastricht and no penalty could be imposed. After the Maastricht Treaty, further proceedings were taken against Greece in *Commission v Greece* (C-387/97). There the CJEU stated:

"The basic criteria which must be taken into account in order to ensure that penalty payments have coercive force and that community law is applied uniformly and effectively are, in principle, the duration

> of the infringement, the degree of seriousness and the ability of the Member State to pay. In applying these criteria regard should be had in particular to the effects of failure to comply on public and private interests and to the urgency of getting the Member State concerned to fulfil its obligations."

The Court imposed a fine of €20,000 for every day from the judgment being passed until the breaches were remedied. This was the first time a fine was imposed. The European Commission had recommended a higher penalty but the Court is not bound by the Commission's proposal.

In *Commission v France* (C-304/02), it was held that both a lump sum fine and periodic penalty payment can be imposed at the same time. Here both were imposed on France for a breach of fisheries legislation which had been condemned in 1991. The reason behind these penalties is not to compensate for the damage caused by the Member State in failing to comply with its European obligations. Instead, it is to put economic pressure on the Member State to remedy the breach.

General Principles of EU Law

9

Introduction

This chapter will analyse a number of general principles of EU law. These are principles of law developed and applied by the Court of Justice of the European Union (CJEU) and the courts of the Member States. They come from the common legal principles of the Member States, European Union law and the European Convention on Human Rights. These principles allow the CJEU to develop, expand and interpret EU law. Laws can be challenged if they go against these principles. Many of these principles are interlinked with one another and it can be difficult at times to draw a line between where one principle ends and another begins. In this chapter, we will look at legal certainty, legitimate expectation, subsidiarity and proportionality. We will also look, where appropriate, at the position of these principles in Irish law.

Legal Certainty

Legal certainty is the legal principle which says that people should be able to know what the law is. The law should be clear and people should be able to know what they can and can't do legally. They should also be able to find out what their rights and obligations are. Legal certainty was one of the first principles of law recognised by the CJEU; it has been a general principle of EU law since the late 1950s when it was first laid out in joined cases *SNUPAT v High Authority of the European Coal and Steel Community* (C-42/59 and 49/59). It was noted by the Court in *Kuhne & Heitz v Produktschap voor Pluimvee en Eiren* (C-453/00) that "[l]egal certainty is one of a number of general principles recognised by Community law". Legal certainty is internationally recognised as a core requirement for the rule of law. It is a general principle of international and public law as well as of EU law, and its existence predates the EU. As such, it covers a number of different legal concepts including legitimate expectations and proportionality. The European Commission has a legal certainty group promoting legal certainty. As can be seen throughout this text, the CJEU seeks to promote legal certainty by ensuring that EU law is applied uniformly and consistently by each of the Member States. It uses a number of different doctrines to do this. In *Heinrich* (C-345/06), the Court held that in EU law

> "the principle of legal certainly requires that Community rules enable those concerned to know precisely the extent of the obligations which are imposed on them. Individuals must be able to ascertain unequivocally what their rights and obligations are and take steps accordingly."

In *Gondrand Frères* (C-169/80), the Court held that

> "[t]he principle of legal certainty requires that rules imposing charges on the taxpayer must be clear and precise so that he may know without ambiguity what are his rights and obligations and may take steps according."

The Court went on to hold that where there are ambiguities or lack of clarity in measures imposing charges, those matters should be resolved in favour of the taxpayers. These dicta were quoted by the Irish High Court in *O'Brien v Ireland* [1991] 2 I.R. 387.

In EU law, the principle of legal certainty prohibits retroactive laws. This means that laws cannot not take effect before they are made. For example, it cannot be made a crime to have done something in the past before the law was created. In *Racke* (C-98/78), the Court held:

> "A fundamental principle in the community legal order requires that a measure adopted by the public authorities shall not be applicable to those concerned before they have the opportunity to make themselves acquainted with it."

In *Gesamthochschule Duisburg v Hauptzollamt München-Mitte* (C-234/83), the Court held that the principle of legal certainty requires that

> "a regulation should not be applied retroactively, regardless of whether such an application might produce favourable or unfavourable effects for the persons concerned, unless a sufficiently clear indication can be found, either in the terms of the regulation or in its stated objectives, that the regulation was not merely providing for the future."

Following on from this, in *Opel Austria v Council* (T-115/94) the Court held that a Regulation did not come into effect until it had been published. Opel had brought the case claiming that the Regulation violated the principle of legal certainty because it legally came into effect before it had been published and before Opel had been notified. It should be noted that the Court in *Decker* (C-99/78) held:

> "Although in general the principle of legal certainty precludes a Community measure from taking effect from a point in time before its publication, it may exceptionally be otherwise where the purpose to be achieved so demands and where the legitimate expectations of those concerned are duly respected."

In *Plantanol* (C-201/08), the Court held:

> "[A]ccording to the case-law, the principle of legal certainty, the corollary of which is the principle of the protection of legitimate expectations, requires, on the one hand, that rules of law must be clear and precise and, on the other, that their application must be foreseeable by those subject to them."

Legal certainty in Ireland

Legal certainty is recognised as a principle of Irish law. Hardiman J. in *People (DPP) v Cagney* [2008] 2 I.R. 111 found that:

> "From a legal and constitutional point of view, it is a fundamental value that a citizen should know, or at least be able to find out, with some considerable measure of certainty, what precisely is prohibited and what is lawful."

In *DPP v Hughes* [2013] 2 I.R. 619, the same judge refused to allow the applicants application to enlarge time in which to appeal a conviction for possessing fire arms and explosives as it would be against the principle of legal certainty. He found that "[n]o system of law could operate if decisions intended to be final could subsequently be set aside on the basis of developments which occurred only after their completion." In *DPP v Douglas* [2013] 2 I.L.R.M. 324, it was found that there is a constitutional entitlement to legal certainty in the sphere of criminal offences. The leading case on legal certainty in Ireland however is *King v Attorney General* [1981] I.R. 233 where the plaintiff successfully challenged the constitutionality of part of s.4 of the Vagrancy Act 1824, which had created the offence of loitering with intent to commit a felony, on the grounds that this was unconstitutionally vague. Henchy J., in the Supreme Court, held:

"The ingredients of the offence and the mode by which its commission may be proved are so arbitrary, so vague, so difficult to rebut, so related to rumour or ill-repute or past conduct, so ambiguous in failing to distinguish between apparent and real behaviour of a criminal nature, so prone to make a man's lawful occasions become unlawful and criminal by the breadth and arbitrariness of the discretion that is vested in both the prosecutor and the judge, so indiscriminately contrived to mark as criminal conduct committed by one person in certain circumstances when the same conduct, when engaged in by another person in similar circumstances, would be free of the taint of criminality, so out of keeping with the basic concept inherent in our legal system that a man may walk abroad in the secure knowledge that he will not be singled out from his fellow-citizens and branded and punished as a criminal unless it has been established beyond reasonable doubt that he has deviated from a clearly prescribed standard of conduct, and generally so singularly at variance with both the explicit and implicit characteristics and limitations of the criminal law as to the onus of proof and mode of proof, that it is not so much a question of ruling unconstitutional the type of offence we are now considering as identifying the particular constitutional provisions with which such an offence is at variance.

Legitimate Expectation

Legitimate expectation was described in *Duff v Minister for Agriculture and Food* (C-63/93) as being a corollary of the doctrine of legal certainty. It is the principle that those who act in good faith on the basis of the law as it is, or as it seems to be, should not be frustrated in their expectations unless there is an overriding public interest. In *Ampafrance* (C-177/99), it was held the principle of the protection of legitimate expectations "appears to be an expression, taking the form of a subjective right, of legal certainty". *Plantanol* shows that legitimate expectation is wrapped up in the doctrine of legal certainty. This doctrine originated in German law where it is known as "*vertraensschutz*", and made its way into EU law and the law of other Member States including Ireland which recognises the precept that legitimate expectations should be protected. This means that once an EU institution has induced a party into taking a particular course of action, it cannot change its position if that would cause the party to suffer loss.

Legitimate expectations arose initially in relation to the revocation of administrative decisions. The majority of the cases in which legitimate expectations have been referred to are about agriculture and the steel industry.

This is because these are both highly regulated industries. In *Deuka v EVGF* (C-78/74), the Court interpreted a regulation in such a way as to protect the legitimate expectations of wheat processors. The leading case on legitimate expectation is *Mulder v Minister van Landbouw en Visserij* (C-120/86). This case was a preliminary ruling in relation to a milk levy. Farmers were paid to stop producing milk in order to reduce the milk surplus. Mr Mulder did this for a five-year period, then tried to resume producing milk without paying a levy. He was refused as this was only available to those who had produced milk the previous year. This had been introduced during the five-year period. He argued that the EU had encouraged him to stop producing milk by offering premiums and that he had a legitimate expectation he could re-enter milk production. It was held that:

> "The regulations on the additional levy on milk were adopted in breach of the principle of protection of legitimate expectations. Those regulations must therefore be declared invalid on that ground, and it is unnecessary to consider the other arguments as to their invalidity."

It is clear that even a regulation, the strongest form of EU law, can be struck down where it breaches a legitimate expectation.

The most comprehensive definition of legitimate expectation was given by the Court in *Branco v Commission* (T-347/03). Eugénio Branco had a contract with the Portuguese authorities to train young adults under the European Social Fund. Due to irregularities in his certification, he was refused a payment and asked to pay back the money he had already received. He appealed, saying that this was contrary to the principle of legitimate expectation due to the fact his work had been certified by the Portuguese authorities before. The General Court held:

> "Three conditions must be satisfied in order to claim entitlement of the protection of the legitimate expectation. First, precise, unconditional and consistent assurances originating from authorized and reliable sources must have been given to the person concerned by the community authorities. Secondly, those assurances must be such give rise to a legitimate expectation on the part of the person to whom they are addressed. Third, the assurances given must comply with the applicable rules."

The Court found that he was not entitled to claim legitimate expectation as he failed to satisfy the first condition. It was for the Commission to decide whether or not to authorise the payment and not the Portuguese authorities and the Commission has given no assurances in this case.

It is worthwhile to look at these three conditions in turn. First, the applicant must have received precise, unconditional and consistent assurances originating from authorised and reliable sources. When looking at these assurances the Court will apply the standard of whether or not a "prudent and discriminating trader" would have foreseen it. In *Van den Bergh en Jurgens BV and Van Dik Food Products (Lopik) BV v Commission* (C-265/85), the Court stated:

> "Any trader in regard to whom an institution has given rise to justified hopes may rely on the principle of the protection of legitimate expectations. On the other hand, if a prudent and discriminating trader could have foreseen the adoption of a Community measure likely to affect his interests, he cannot plead that principle if the measure is adopted."

An example of a case where an expectation was found to be legitimate is *CIRFS* (C-313/90), where the CJEU found the European Commission was bound by the terms of its policy framework. In *Ijssel-Vliet* (C-311/94), it was held that Commission guidelines were binding on the Dutch Government when they had been built into a Dutch aid scheme.

Secondly, those assurances must give rise to a legitimate expectation on the part of the person to whom they are addressed. A claim will fail if the expectation is not legitimate. For example, in the case of *Sonasa* (T-126-97), the applicant had not met the conditions required for particular funding. His claim to have an expectation of that funding could therefore not be legitimate.

Thirdly, the assurances given must comply with the applicable rules. The Court in *Branco* drew here from *Forvass* v *Commission* (T-203/97) and *G v Commission* (T-199/01), which in turn drew from *Chomel v Commission* (T-123/89). There the Court held:

> "With regard to the alleged breach of the principle of proper administration and of the duty to have regard for officials' interests, it must be pointed out that the protection of the rights and interests of officials must always be subject to compliance with the legal rules currently in force; a mere request, made on acceptance of an offer of employment, for a right to be granted can never give rise to the granting of that right, contrary to the Staff Regulations, merely on the ground that the administration did not respond to the request before the official entered the service. It follows that the claim that the Commission failed to consider all the relevant facts and to take account of either the interests of the service or those of the official concerned cannot be accepted."

This means that all appropriate rules must be complied with and the expectation must be legitimate. In *Wasmeier v Commission of the European Communities* (T-381/00), it was held that the information contained in a competition notice is, in principle, too general and conditional to be capable of justifying a legitimate expectation.

Even if there is a legitimate expectation, it may also fail if there is an overriding public interest which overrides the interest in preserving the expectation. It is for the defendant in the case to prove that this overriding public interest exists. It was held in *CNTA* (C-74/74) that the Court will enquire if the public interest overrides the legitimate expectation.

Legitimate expectation in Ireland

In Ireland, legitimate expectation is a legal principal that arises in contract law, administrative law and constitutional law. Legitimate expectation entered Irish law in the landmark case of *Webb v Ireland* [1988] I.R. 353 which arose out of the discovery of a hoard of treasure in Derrynaflan, Co. Tipperary. Legitimate expectation is the doctrine of law which applies the principles of fairness and reasonableness to the situation where an applicant has an interest in a public body complying with an undertaking or keeping up a long-standing practice. If a legitimate expectation has been breached, a public body can be compelled to follow certain procedural steps, either because it has done so in the past or because it has indicated to the person that such a procedure would be followed in his or her case. It is a purely administrative remedy; it only applies to public bodies and cannot be used between two private parties. The current leading case on legitimate expectation is *Glencar Exploration v Mayo County Council* [2002] 1 I.R. 84. There, Fennelly J. set out a three-step test, similar to that in EU law, which must be met for a legitimate expectation to arise.

1. "[T]he public authority must have made a statement or adopted a position amounting to a promise or representation, express or implied, as to how it will act in respect of an identifiable area of its activity."
2. "[T]he representation must be addressed or conveyed either directly or indirectly to an identifiable person or group of persons, affected actually or potentially, in such a way that it forms part of a transaction definitively entered into or a relationship between that person and group and the public authority or that the person or group had acted on the faith of the representation."
3. "[I]t must be such as to create an expectation reasonably entertained by the person or group that the public authority will abide by the representation to the extent that it would be unjust to permit the public authority to resile from it."

Subsidiarity and Proportionality

Subsidiarity and proportionality are very closely interlinked. They deal with how power is divided between the EU and its Member States. They govern who should have the power to make legislation and how much force should go into that legislation. These two topics are very closely related and will be examined together as proportionality makes up a part of the test for subsidiarity. In these topics, we will be looking at EU competences. Article 5(1) of the TEU states:

> "The limits of Union competences are governed by the principle of conferral. The use of Union competences is governed by the principles of subsidiarity and proportionality."

As we have seen before, the Member States surrender their power in various competences to the EU through the Treaties. The European Union only has those powers that are conferred on it and has no powers as of right. Article 5(2) of the TEU describes the principle of conferral as follows:

> "Under the principle of conferral, the Union shall act only within the limits of the competences conferred upon it by the Member States in the Treaties to attain the objectives set out therein. Competences not conferred upon the Union in the Treaties remain with the Member States."

The principle that the EU institutions cannot act beyond the competences conferred up them is also discussed when looking at ultra vires acts in Ch.7—Judicial Review of European Union Law. Subsidiarity is the principle which says that in the area of its non-exclusive competences, the EU may act only if the objective of a proposed action could be better achieved at EU-level than by the Member States. Proportionality is the principle which says that EU action may not go beyond what is necessary to achieve the objectives of the Treaties.

Subsidiarity

The principle of subsidiarity is fundamental to how the EU functions and makes decisions. It decides when the EU is competent to legislate, and contributes to decisions being taken as closely as possible to citizens. Article 5(3) TFEU states:

"Under the principle of subsidiarity, in areas which do not fall within its exclusive competence, the Union shall act only if and in so far as the objectives of the proposed action cannot be sufficiently achieved by the Member States, either at central level or at regional and local level, but can rather, by reason of the scale or effects of the proposed action, be better achieved at Union level.

The institutions of the Union shall apply the principle of subsidiarity as laid down in the Protocol on the application of the principles of subsidiarity and proportionality. National Parliaments ensure compliance with the principle of subsidiarity in accordance with the procedure set out in that Protocol."

According to the principle of subsidiarity, the EU can only make laws in areas where it does not have exclusive competence when the action of individual Member States is insufficient or the EU is better placed to do so because of the scale or effects of the proposed action. In other words, this principle means that the EU should not get involved in things that are not its business. The EU has not completely taken over the running of the Member States. The subsidiarity principle was first made a treaty provision by the Maastricht Treaty. This area has guidance in the form of the Protocol on the application of the principles of subsidiarity and proportionality (No. 2). This Protocol requires EU legislation to be drafted with regard to the principles of subsidiarity and proportionality. It gives the Member States an opportunity to raise any objections they have based on these principles. This principle, unlike the other principles discussed in this chapter, is purely one of European law.

As we have seen in Ch.3 (Sources and Types of EU Law), the EU only has competence in areas where it has been given power by the Member States. The EU's competences are set out in the EU Treaties. The EU can only act within the competences conferred on it by the Treaties, and where the Treaties do not confer competences on the EU, they remain with the Member States. There are three different types of competence: exclusive, shared and supporting. Only the EU can act in areas where it has exclusive competence, such as the Customs Union. In areas of shared competence, such as the Single Market, either the EU or the Member States may act, but the Member States cannot act once the EU has done so. In areas of supporting competence, such as culture, tourism and education, both the EU and the Member States can act and the Member States are not prevented from taking action if the EU has acted. The principle of subsidiarity applies to areas of shared and supporting competences.

The principle of subsidiarity applies to all of the European Union institutions, although the rule has most significance in terms of legislation. Both the parliaments of the Member States and the Court of Justice monitor compliance with the principle of subsidiarity. The Court of Justice decides whether an act falls within the exclusive competence of the EU.

Subsidiarity embraces three separate, but related, concepts:

1. The EU can only take action if the objectives of that action cannot be sufficiently achieved by the Member States.
2. The EU is better placed to take the action because of its scale or effects.
3. If the EU does take action, it should not go beyond what is necessary to achieve the Treaty objective.

The first two parts are called "the test of comparative efficiency". The third part is a proportionality test.

PROPORTIONALITY

Proportionality is a fundamental principle of European law. It states that the European Union can only act to the level that is needed to achieve its objectives and no further. Proportionality, like legitimate expectation, is a legal principle that had its origins in German law, but which has since spread to the other EU Member States, including Ireland. It is worth noting that in *Internationale Handelsgesellschaft* (C-11/70), which states EU law is superior even to constitutional law, the German courts were trying to strike down an EU law for violating this principle. Proportionality requires that there is a balance between the public interest achieved by an act which affects someone's rights and the adverse effects which are caused by the act. It requires that an action be no more than is needed to achieve the intended objective. This means that the need for action, and the costs and benefits expected from that action, must be examined. It is very closely linked in EU law with the principle of subsidiarity. Both of these principles put limits on the amount of power that authorities can wield. It also appears in other areas of EU law, such as the exceptions to the freedom of movement. Like other EU legal principles, proportionality entered EU law through the decisions of the Court of Justice. It is now found in art.5(4) TEU which states:

> "Under the principle of proportionality, the content and form of Union action shall not exceed what is necessary to achieve the objectives of the Treaties.
>
> The institutions of the Union shall apply the principle of proportionality as laid down in the Protocol on the application of the principles of subsidiarity and proportionality."

Administrative measures must not be arbitrary, unfair or based on irrational considerations. Proportionality is, at one level, an expression of simple common sense; you don't use a sledgehammer to crack a nut. For example, if the EU was worried about littering, and introduced a Directive requiring the Member States to bring in the death penalty for anyone caught littering, this would clearly be disproportionate as the measure goes far in excess of what is needed to tackle the problem (notwithstanding the other legal problems this would bring).

Proportionality has been found to be a general principle of EU law in a number of decisions. In *Fedesa* (C-331/88), the Court stated:

> "The Court has consistently held that the principle of proportionality is one of the general principles of Community law. By virtue of that principle, the lawfulness of the prohibition of an economic activity is subject to the condition that the prohibitory measures are appropriate and necessary in order to achieve the objectives legitimately pursued by the legislation in question; when there is a choice between several appropriate measures recourse must be had to the least onerous, and the disadvantages caused must not be disproportionate to the aims pursued."

In this case, a total ban on hormonal substances in livestock farming due to potential dangers was upheld as proportionate, even taking into account the substantial negative financial consequences for some traders. The Court found that it would only interfere in policy judgments on grounds of proportionality where the action was manifestly inappropriate. In *Internationale Handelsgesellschaft*, the Court found both fundamental rights and proportionality to be principles of EU law.

In EU law, there are four stages to the proportionality test:

1. The measure must have a legitimate aim;
2. The measure must be suitable to achieve the aim;
3. The measure must be necessary to achieve the aim, i.e. there cannot be any easier way of doing it; and
4. The measure must be reasonable, considering the competing interests of different groups at hand.

These last two criteria are often merged into one by the Court of Justice, depending on the margin of discretion that the Court sees as being afforded to the Member State.

A number of EU acts have been struck down as being disproportionate. One example was *Man Sugar* (C-181/84), where the claimant forfeited

£1,670,370 in security when their application for a licence was a few hours late due to an error. This was held to be disproportionate. In *ABNA v Minister for Health* (C-11/04), an EU Directive required manufacturers of animal feed to indicate, at a customer's request, the exact composition of the feed. This was struck down as unnecessary to protect health, and going beyond what was required to protect health.

In *Affish* (C-183/95), an EU Decision totally banning the importation of Japanese fish on health grounds was upheld. Even though not all Japanese fish factories had hygiene problems and measures short of a ban were available, the Court thought it would not be practical to check the hygiene of all Japanese fish factories and that a reasonably representative sample had been checked. Therefore, the ban was found to be proportionate.

National parliaments can also now check compliance with the principles of subsidiarity and proportionality. For this purpose, an early warning system has been introduced through the Protocol. This allows national parliaments to issue a reasoned position setting out why the legislative proposal does not meet the subsidiarity and proportionality requirements. If this reasoned position is supported, the legislative proposal must be reviewed again by the institution that issued it. Following this review, the proposal can be kept, amended or withdrawn. If the European Commission decides to keep the draft, it must issue a reasoned opinion, stating why it considers the draft to follow the subsidiarity principle. If a majority of the Members of the Council of the EU or a majority of the votes cast in the European Parliament are of the opinion that the proposal does not comply with the subsidiarity principle, then it is not examined any further.

Proportionality in Ireland

The proportionality principle is of increased importance in Ireland due to the Supreme Court decision in *Meadows v Minister for Justice, Equality and Law Reform* [2010] 2 I.R. 701. In *Heaney v Ireland* [1994] 3 I.R. 593, the High Court adopted a three-part test for assessing if a measure was proportionate. It must:

1. be rationally connected to the objective and not be arbitrary, unfair or based on irrational considerations;
2. impair the right as little as possible; and
3. be such that their effects on rights are proportional to the objective.

Unfortunately, the test in Ireland is now less clear thanks to the decision in *Meadows* which tied proportionality in with the duty to act reasonably.

O'Donnell J. observed in *Nottinghamshire County Council v K.B.* [2013] 4 I.R. 662:

> "It has now become common place to refer to proportionality in constitutional litigation. I think it is necessary however to recognise that proportionality in itself is not an entirely transparent concept. It can be applied strictly to strike down legislation or generously to sustain it. It is important to remember that proportionality is a tool for analysis, rather than an end in itself. The mere statement that something is *proportionate* is almost as delphic as the statement that it is *reasonable*. The analysis of whether any particular restriction or limitation is consistent to the Constitution may be assisted by the structure proportionality analysis provides, but only if it is explained *why* any particular provision is permitted by the Constitution, and is proportionate. In my view it is an error to approach the constitutional issue by simply asking, almost in the abstract, whether any particular provision is proportionate as an almost self-standing test of constitutionality and detached from careful consideration of the text and the values necessarily implied by it" (emphasis in original).

10 EU Citizenship

Introduction

Every national of an EU Member State is a citizen of the EU. EU citizenship does not replace national citizenship: it is additional to it. In *Grzelczyk* (C-184/99), the Court of Justice held that "Union citizenship is destined to be the fundamental status of nationals of the Member States." Union citizenship gives extra rights to citizens of Member States and their families. It was not provided for in the founding treaties but was introduced with the Maastricht Treaty and is a rapidly expanding area of law. EU Citizenship is governed by arts 20–25 TFEU, the Citizenship Directive (Directive 2004/38) and the case law of the Court of Justice. Article 20 gives the basis of EU citizenship:

> "1. Citizenship of the Union is hereby established. Every person holding the nationality of a Member State shall be a citizen of the Union. Citizenship of the Union shall be additional to and not replace national citizenship.
>
> 2. Citizens of the Union shall enjoy the rights and be subject to the duties provided for in the Treaties. They shall have, inter alia:
>
> (a) the right to move and reside freely within the territory of the Member States;
>
> (b) the right to vote and to stand as candidates in elections to the European Parliament and in municipal elections in their Member State of residence, under the same conditions as nationals of that State;
>
> (c) the right to enjoy, in the territory of a third country in which the Member State of which they are nationals is not represented, the protection of the diplomatic and consular authorities of any Member State on the same conditions as the nationals of that State;
>
> (d) the right to petition the European Parliament, to apply to the European Ombudsman, and to address the institutions and advisory bodies of the Union in any of the Treaty languages and to obtain a reply in the same language.
>
> These rights shall be exercised in accordance with the conditions and limits defined by the Treaties and by the measures adopted thereunder."

EU citizenship rights only apply when moving to another Member State: they do not arise in a national's home State.

EU citizenship depends on a person's nationality of a Member State. This means that Member States control EU citizenship by controlling who their nationals are. Although EU law does not control how Member States grant nationality, it requires them to recognise nationality granted by other Member States. This arose in *Micheletti v Delegación del Gobierno Cantabria* (C-369/90). In this case, Mr Micheletti had dual Italian/Argentine nationality. Before moving to Spain, he lived in Argentina. Under Spanish law, foreigners were treated as being from their place of habitual residence. The Spanish authorities therefore treated him as an Argentinian, not an Italian, and therefore not an EU Citizen. The CJEU held that it was not open to a Member State to refuse to recognise nationality of another Member State because this would undermine the rights and freedoms associated with EU citizenship.

In *Rottmann* (C-135/08), it was held that EU citizenship can be lost through deception. There Dr Janko Rottmann had acquired German nationality and, in doing so, lost his Austrian nationality. He was stripped of his German nationality when it emerged he had lied to the German authorities about a pending criminal fraud case against him in Austria. It was held that this had the effect of depriving him of his EU citizenship but that the German authorities were permitted to do this because states can withdraw nationality when it is granted on the basis of fraud.

The Right of EU Citizens to Move to other States

The right of EU citizens to move and reside in other EU States is one of the most important EU citizenship rights. The EU estimates that 13 million EU citizens now live in other EU Member States. This right is stated in both art.20(2)(a) and 21 TFEU. Article 21(1) TFEU provides:

> "Every citizen of the Union shall have the right to move and reside freely within the territory of the Member States, subject to the limitations and conditions laid down in the Treaties and by the measures adopted to give them effect."

Before EU citizenship was created, provisions on free movement of workers and self-employed persons could be found in the Treaties. However, these provisions generally only conferred rights on people moving to work. In the 1990s, three residency directives were adopted which gave rights to non-economic migrants. The Citizenship Directive (Directive 2004/38) now gives this right to EU citizens, whether they are working or not, and it also extends rights to their families even if they are not also EU citizens.

The Citizenship Directive

Directive 2004/38, also known as the Citizenship Directive, was adopted in 2004. It consolidated almost all existing legislation on free movement of persons and provides a legislative framework for the rights of EU citizens and their families. This Directive is implemented in Ireland by the European Communities (Free Movement of Persons) Regulations 2015. Article 3(1) provides that the Citizenship Directive applies to "all Union citizens who move to or reside in a Member State other than that of which they are a national, and to their family members ... who accompany them."

Under art.2(2), "family member" means:

a) the spouse;
b) the civil partner;
c) direct descendants or the spouse's dependants who are under the age of 21;
d) the dependent parents, grandparents, etc. and those of the spouse.

Article 3(2) requires the host Member State to facilitate the entry of other family members not included in art.2(2). In *Rahman* (C-83/11), the Court of Justice held that Member States are not required to grant every application for residence or entry made by family members of EU citizens who do not fall under art.2(2), even if they are dependent on that citizen. However, the Court found that Member States must ensure that their legislation contains criteria which gives applicants the right to a decision based on examination of their personal circumstances, and a right to the reasons why if they are refused. The Court held that Member States have a wide discretion when selecting these criteria. The Court found in *Carpenter* (C-60/00) that an EU citizen in another Member State might be able to rely on the Treaty rules on free movement in order to secure the entry and residence of a third-country national family member in their home state. Article 5 sets out the right of entry and forbids visa requirements except for certain third-country nationals. All that is required for entry is a passport or national identity card.

Residency

Time limits for residence

The Citizenship Directive provides for three different periods of residence: up to three months; longer than three months; and permanent residence.

Three-month right of residence

Article 6 of the Citizenship Directive provides:

> "Union citizens shall have the right of residence on the territory of another Member State for a period of up to three months without any conditions or any formalities other than the requirement to hold a valid identity card or passport."

Article 6(2) extends this right to family members who have a valid passport and are accompanying or joining the EU citizen. The Citizenship Directive also puts limits on this right. Article 14(1) provides that the right of temporary residence is only as long as the EU citizen and his or her family do not become an unreasonable burden on the social assistance of the Member State. Article 24(2) provides that Member States are not obliged to provide social assistance during the first three months of residence.

Right of residence for over three months

Article 7 of the Citizenship Directive concerns the right of residence for more than three months. This article provides EU citizens with the right of residence in another Member State for longer than three months if they:

a) are workers or self-employed persons in the Member State; or
b) have sufficient resources for themselves and their family members, have comprehensive health insurance and do not become a burden on the social assistance system of the Member State; or
c) are studying and have comprehensive health insurance (they must assure the national authorities by means of a declaration that they have sufficient resources for themselves and their family members that they will not become a burden on the social assistance system of the Member State); or
d) are family members accompanying or joining an EU citizen who satisfies the above conditions.

Permanent residence

The Citizenship Directive also contains a right of permanent residence in another Member State under art.16. This right is gained after five years of residence in a host Member State. However, it is possible to gain permanent residence more quickly under certain conditions laid out in art.17. For example, under art.17(1), people retiring can get it after three years. Once acquired, the right of permanent residence is only lost through absence from the host Member State for a period exceeding two consecutive years. It was held in *Onuekwere v Secretary of State for the Home Department* (C-378/12) that time spent in prison does not count towards this.

Residency Requirements

Certain conditions apply to the residency of non-working citizens which do not apply to workers. For the first three months, non-workers may not be an "unreasonable burden" on the host State's social assistance. Residence for longer than three months requires them to have sufficient resources not to become a burden on the host State, together with comprehensive sickness insurance. This reflects the fact that the right of free movement originally applied to workers, not everyone. The EU particularly wants to make it easy for workers to move around. In terms of what are sufficient resources, art.8(4) of the Citizenship Directive provides:

> "Member States may not lay down a fixed amount which they regard as 'sufficient resources', but they must take into account the personal situation of the person concerned. In all cases this amount shall not be higher than the threshold below which nationals of the host Member State become eligible for social assistance, or, where this criterion is not applicable, higher than the minimum social security pension paid by the host Member State."

Proportionality

The CJEU has held that the principle of proportionality applies to residency requirements. In *Baumbast* (C-413/99), the applicant was a German married to a Colombian. They had lived together in the UK since 1990 with their two children who had dual nationality. He had been a worker and later became self-employed. Unfortunately, his company did not succeed. From 1993, he worked for German companies abroad while his family stayed in the UK. The family had German health insurance, and did not receive social assistance. In 1995, the Home Secretary refused to renew their residence permit because the residency requirements were not met. A tribunal held he was not a worker, and was not covered by the Directive in force at the time (which had similar requirements to those in the Citizenship Directive). Further, it held that the family's health insurance was insufficient because it would not cover emergency medical treatment in the UK. The CJEU held that the residency requirements were subject to the principle of proportionality. The Court found that he had worked and lawfully resided in the UK for several years and during that period his family also lived there and remained there, even after his activities in the State came to an end. It also found that as he had sufficient resources to look after his family, neither he, nor his family, had become an unreasonable burden and that they had German health insurance. It held that: "Under those circumstances, to refuse to allow him to exercise the right of residence on the ground that his sickness insurance does not cover the emergency treatment was disproportionate."

In *Zhu and Chen v Secretary of State for the Home Department* (C-200/02), Mrs Chen was a Chinese national working in the UK. She moved to Northern Ireland to have a baby (Catherine), so that the child would have Irish nationality. At the time, children born on the island of Ireland automatically gained Irish nationality regardless of their ancestry. This was later changed in 2004 following the twenty-seventh amendment to the Constitution, following concerns that it was being abused. EU citizens cannot use their citizenship rights in their own State, these rights only arise when moving to another state. If Catherine had been born in the UK and had English nationality, she would not have been able to rely on citizenship rights.

The Home Secretary refused Mrs Chen and Catherine long-term residence permits because it was thought that she was not protected by EU law, and that Catherine was not exercising EU rights. However, she had health insurance and sufficient resources to prevent either herself or Catherine from becoming an unreasonable burden. The CJEU held that Catherine did have a right of residence in the UK on the basis of her Irish citizenship. The Court also held it was clear that Catherine had sufficient resources and health insurance, provided by her mother, to prevent her from becoming an unreasonable burden.

Wholly Internal Situations, or Reverse Discrimination

Under art.3, the Citizenship Directive applies to European Union citizens who move to or reside in a Member State other than that of which they are a national. This means you cannot rely on this Directive in your national State. The Court, on occasion, has to consider whether a case was "wholly internal" to the Member State, or whether there was a cross-border element. In wholly internal situations, only the law of the Member State applies and EU law does not. This means that if a case is wholly internal, you would not be able to rely on free movement rights. This is sometimes also referred to as reverse discrimination.

An example of a wholly internal situation is *Morson and Jhanjan v The Netherlands* (C-35 and 36/82). There Surinamese nationals wanted to stay in the Netherlands with their Dutch son, who worked there. He had not exercised his free movement rights so there was no cross-border element. The CJEU held that it was a "wholly internal situation" and was therefore governed by the law of the Netherlands, not EU law.

In *Garcia Avello v Belgium* (C-148/02), a Spaniard and his Belgian wife lived in Belgium with their two children. Their children had dual Spanish and Belgian nationality. Belgian law required that the children take their father's surname but they wanted to add their mother's, which was the custom in Spain. They challenged this law. The Court held that although rules governing registration of surnames fell within national competence, the fact that an EU citizen's children were living in another Member State was enough to provide a link to EU law which stopped the case being "wholly internal" to Belgium. This means that the Treaty provisions on EU citizenship conferred rights on applicants who had never left the Member State in which they had been born. In these cases, they were claiming a different Member State's nationality to their host Member State.

In *Schempp v Finanzamt München* (C-403/03), the Court held that it was not a wholly internal situation where maintenance was paid to a spouse who had moved to another Member State. Although the applicant had not exercised his freedom of movement, the fact that the maintenance went abroad affected his taxes in Germany.

One of the landmark cases in this area is *Ruiz Zambrano* (C-34/09). In this case, the CJEU considered the status of non-EU parents of EU-citizen children who had never left their Member State. Eight Member States, including Ireland, intervened in the *Zambrano* case to argue that EU law on citizenship should not apply as this was a "wholly internal" situation. The CJEU disagreed and found that the Treaties preclude measures which have the effect of depriving citizens of "the genuine enjoyment of the substance of the rights conferred by virtue of their status as citizens".

The Zambranos were a Colombian couple who sought asylum in Belgium after their eldest son had been kidnapped in Colombia. They were refused asylum, but the Belgian authorities accepted that they could not be returned to Colombia due to the principle of non-refoulment—the principle of international law that says victims of persecution should not be returned to their persecutors. While they waited for their applications to be processed, Mr Zambrano started working (despite not having a work permit), and Mrs Zambrano gave birth to two children who were granted Belgian nationality. When their first child was born, Mr Zambrano had sufficient resources to provide for the family and paid income tax on his salary. He later became unemployed and applied for social assistance. This application and the couple's applications for residency as parents of Belgian nationals were refused. When the Zambranos challenged these decisions, the question of whether EU law applied, or if it was a wholly internal situation was raised as the children had never exercised their free movement rights. The Court held:

> "In those circumstances, Article 20 TFEU precludes national measures which have the effect of depriving citizens of the Union of the genuine enjoyment of the substance of the rights conferred by virtue of their status as citizens of the Union (see, to that effect, C-135/08 *Rottmann*).
>
> A refusal to grant a right of residence to a third country national with dependent minor children in the Member State where those children are nationals and reside, and also a refusal to grant such a person a work permit, has such an effect.
>
> It must be assumed that such a refusal would lead to a situation where those children, citizens of the Union, would have to leave the territory of the Union in order to accompany their parents. Similarly, if a work permit were not granted to such a person, he would risk not having sufficient resources to provide for himself and his family, which would also result in the children, citizens of the Union, having to leave the territory of the Union. In those circumstances, those citizens of the Union would, in fact, be unable to exercise the substance of the rights conferred on them by virtue of their status as citizens of the Union.
>
> Accordingly, the answer to the questions referred is that Article 20 TFEU is to be interpreted as meaning that it precludes a Member State from refusing a third country national upon whom his minor children, who are European Union citizens, are dependent, a right of residence in the Member State of residence and nationality of those children, and from refusing to grant a work permit to that third country national, in so far as such decisions deprive those children of the genuine enjoyment of the substance of the rights attaching to the status of European Union citizen."

Although there was no cross-border element to the case, forcing the parents of EU Citizens to leave Belgium would have resulted in depriving those citizens of the substance of their EU rights.

Zambrano can be compared to *McCarthy v Secretary of State for the Home Department* (C-434/09). Mrs McCarthy had always lived in the UK but had dual Irish and UK nationality. She sought a right of residence in the UK as an Irish national so that her Jamaican husband could get derivative rights as the spouse of an EU citizen and stay with her in the UK. Mrs McCarthy received state benefits and was neither economically active nor self-sufficient. Article 3(1) provides that the Citizenship Directive only applies to countries other than that of a national, so the husband could not get any derivative EU citizenship rights under it in the UK by being married to a UK national. The

Court of Justice held that the Citizenship Directive did not apply in this case, as McCarthy had always resided in the Member State of which she was a national and had never exercised her free movement rights. The Court found that, in contrast to the *Zambrano* case, EU law did not apply, because the failure by British authorities to consider her Irish nationality did not affect her right to remain in the UK or her right to freedom of movement, nor did it deprive her of the substance of her rights. It was a matter for national law. Accordingly, her husband could not benefit from the rights under the Citizenship Directive. McCarthy's personal situation can be contrasted with the Zambrano children. They were infants who were completely dependent on their parents, while she was an adult who was not dependent on her husband. If these young children were separated from their parents, it would cause them huge difficulties which would not arise in McCarthy's case. It is easy to see why the Court was more prepared to allow her to be separated from her husband than the children from their parents as this would not have the effect of depriving her of the genuine enjoyment of the substance of her rights as a citizen.

The "genuine enjoyment of the substance of EU rights" test was clarified in *Dereci v Bundesministerium für Inneres* (C-256/11). There, five third-country nationals wanted to reside with Austrian family members who had never exercised their right to free movement and who did not rely them for maintenance. The Court held:

> "As nationals of a Member State, family members of the applicants in the main proceedings enjoy the status of Union citizens under Article 20(1) TFEU and may therefore rely on the rights pertaining to that status, including against their Member State of origin (see *McCarthy*, paragraph 48).
>
> On this basis, the Court has held that Article 20 TFEU precludes national measures which have the effect of depriving Union citizens of the genuine enjoyment of the substance of the rights conferred by virtue of that status (see *Ruiz Zambrano*, paragraph 42).
>
> Indeed, in the case leading to that judgment, the question arose as to whether a refusal to grant a right of residence to a third country national with dependent minor children in the Member State where those children are nationals and reside and a refusal to grant such a person a work permit have such an effect. The Court considered in particular that such a refusal would lead to a situation where those children, who are citizens of the Union, would have to leave the territory of the Union in order to accompany their parents. In those circumstances, those citizens of the Union would, in fact, be unable to exercise the substance of the rights conferred on them by virtue of their status as citizens of the Union (see *Ruiz Zambrano*, paragraphs 43 and 44).

It follows that the criterion relating to the denial of the genuine enjoyment of the substance of the rights conferred by virtue of European Union citizen status refers to situations in which the Union citizen has, in fact, to leave not only the territory of the Member State of which he is a national but also the territory of the Union as a whole.

That criterion is specific in character inasmuch as it relates to situations in which, although subordinate legislation on the right of residence of third country nationals is not applicable, a right of residence may not, exceptionally, be refused to a third country national, who is a family member of a Member State national, as the effectiveness of Union citizenship enjoyed by that national would otherwise be undermined.

Consequently, the mere fact that it might appear desirable to a national of a Member State, for economic reasons or in order to keep his family together in the territory of the Union, for the members of his family who do not have the nationality of a Member State to be able to reside with him in the territory of the Union, is not sufficient in itself to support the view that the Union citizen will be forced to leave Union territory if such a right is not granted.

... In the light of the foregoing observations the answer to the first question is that European Union law and, in particular, its provisions on citizenship of the Union, must be interpreted as meaning that it does not preclude a Member State from refusing to allow a third country national to reside on its territory, where that third country national wishes to reside with a member of his family who is a citizen of the Union residing in the Member State of which he has nationality, who has never exercised his right to freedom of movement, provided that such refusal does not lead, for the Union citizen concerned, to the denial of the genuine enjoyment of the substance of the rights conferred by virtue of his status as a citizen of the Union, which is a matter for the referring court to verify."

Therefore, the *Derechi* judgment confirms the *McCarthy* decision that citizenship provisions can be relied upon by EU citizens who have not exercised their free movement rights, but only so far as the genuine enjoyment of the substance of their EU citizenship rights is not denied. In the case of *Lida v Stadt Ulma* (C-40/11), it was clarified that there are two routes through which EU citizenship rights engage EU law: either where there is cross-border movement to other Member States or where the fundamental status of EU citizenship is endangered, because an EU citizen has been precluded from the genuine enjoyment of the substance of their rights as a citizen. In the case, art.20 applies, although the CJEU takes a more restrictive approach. It requires it to be impossible to remain within the territory of the EU.

Restrictions

Under art.27, citizens and their family members' free movement rights can be restricted on grounds of public policy, security or health, although this cannot be used for economic reasons. "Measures" can include: refusal of entry, refusal of exit, expulsion and territorial restrictions. Measures on the grounds of public policy or security must be proportionate and based exclusively on personal conduct. There must be notice in writing under art.30 and the possibility of review or appeal under art.31. In *Jipa* (C-33/07), the Court found that a state can restrict the movement of its own citizens. A Member State has a right to determine its own policy and security requirements. However, a restriction can only be justified where the personal conduct of the individual constitutes a genuine, present and sufficiently serious threat to one of the fundamental interests of society and complies with the principal of proportionality.

These public policy, security and health exceptions are analysed in more detail in Ch.12—Freedom of Establishment and Free Movement of Services and Capital.

Non-Discrimination and Benefits

Under art.18 TFEU, any discrimination on grounds of nationality is prohibited. Article 24 of the Citizenship Directive concerns the right to equal treatment of EU citizens in host Member States. It provides that

> "all Union citizens residing on the basis of this Directive in the territory of the host Member State shall enjoy equal treatment with the nationals of that Member State within the scope of the Treaty."

This right extends to family members. Article 24(2) notes, however, that Member States are not required to give social assistance in the first three months or maintenance grants until permanent residence is acquired.

In *Martinez Sala v Freistaat Bayern* (C-85/96), the requirement of a residence permit to receive a benefit was found to be discriminatory, because nationals of the Member State were not subject to that same requirement. Therefore, so long as an EU national is lawfully resident within another Member State, they are entitled to equal treatment with nationals of that Member State in respect of benefits falling within the scope of the Treaty.

Students

Education and social policies are matters of national competence. However, the Union citizenship provisions have changed this position. In *Grzelczyk*, a

French national studying in Belgium worked part-time in his first three years of education, but in his final year, he sought a subsistence allowance. He was initially granted this but it was then withdrawn on the basis he was not a Belgian national. The CJEU decided this case on the basis of citizenship and found that he had been discriminated against on the basis of his nationality, which is forbidden by the Treaties. The Court noted that assistance for students had previously fallen outside the Treaties but citizenship rights mean that students who study in other Member States could not be discriminated against. Further, the Court held that getting social assistance in these circumstances could not result in a student's residence permit being withdrawn or non-renewed, although a Member State can do so if the student no longer fulfilled the residency requirements. The CJEU found that the provisions on non-discrimination and European citizenship prevent entitlement to social benefits from being made conditional criteria which don't need to be satisfied by nationals of the host Member State.

Similarly, in *Bidar v London Borough of Ealing* (C-209/03), a French national living in London with his grandmother sought a subsidised loan to continue his studies. Despite having attended secondary school in the UK, this application was refused on the basis that Bidar did not satisfy a three-year residence requirement because time in education was not included under UK national law. Bidar argued that, as an EU citizen, he was entitled to a student loan on an equal basis with any British national. The CJEU agreed with this argument.

Article 24 of the Citizenship Directive does not exclude students from the right to equal treatment in respect of social assistance so long as the student does not become an unreasonable burden. If this occurs, the student may lawfully lose his or her residency entitlements.

Further, art.24(2) of the Citizenship Directive permits Member States to refuse maintenance grants and loans to economically inactive EU citizens who are not permanent residents. In *Förster v Hoofddirective van de Informatia Beheer Groep* (C-158/07), the CJEU upheld a Dutch law requiring a five-year residence period before a maintenance grant would be given to a student from another Member State because it found that it "did not go beyond what was necessary to attain the objective of ensuring that students from other Member States are to a certain degree integrated into the society of the host Member State." This may seem contrary to *Bidar*, but the Court distinguished that case on the basis that the rule sought to be imposed in the UK made it impossible to qualify for a maintenance loan or grant irrespective of how integrated the EU citizen in question was in the host Member State.

POLITICAL RIGHTS OF CITIZENSHIP

Political rights of citizenship can be found in arts 22–24 TFEU.

Under art.22, every EU citizen can vote and stand in municipal elections and in elections to the European Parliament in Member States where they are not nationals. This applies under the same conditions as nationals of that Member State.

Under art.23, every EU citizen is entitled to diplomatic or consular assistance from any Member State when they are in the territory of a third country in which their Member State is not represented.

Article 24 contains a number of rights. It provides for the citizens' initiative which allows EU citizens to participate directly in the development of EU policies, by calling on the European Commission to make legislative proposals. It gives EU citizens the right to petition the European Parliament and to apply to the Ombudsman. It also gives the citizens the right to write to any of the institutions of the EU in any of the official languages of the EU and have an answer in the same language.

In *Delevinge* (C-650/13), a Frenchman was stripped of his voting rights after being convicted of murder. He took a case saying this infringed his citizenship rights and his rights under the Charter of Fundamental Rights. The Court found that the Charter applied but that the French law was a permissible limitation on the rights contained in the Charter.

Free Movement of Persons 11

Introduction

The right to freedom of movement is one of the four freedoms. It allows citizens to move to, live in and, in some cases, access the social welfare system of other EU Member States. It was one of the founding principles of the EU and was originally designed to support the economies of EU countries by providing a mobile work force. The EU estimates that more than a billion trips are made annually within the EU for business or tourism. This right has both vertical and horizontal direct effect. Originally, free movement of persons only applied to workers, but now it applies to non-economically active persons as well; there is a lot of crossover between this topic and EU citizenship.

The right to free movement is protected by the Treaties as well as by Directives and Regulations. It was first provided for in 1951 by the Treaty of Paris, which established the European Coal and Steel Community and provided a right to free movement for workers in those industries. Article 3.2 of the TEU, which contains the aims of the EU, now states:

> "The Union shall offer its citizens an area of freedom, security and justice without internal frontiers, in which the free movement of persons is ensured in conjunction with appropriate measures with respect to external border controls, asylum, immigration and the prevention and combating of crime."

Article 20 TFEU, which deals with the rights of citizens of the EU, notes:

> "Citizens of the Union shall enjoy the rights and be subject to the duties provided for in the Treaties. They shall have, *inter alia*:
> (a) the right to move and reside freely within the territory of the Member States".

The right to free movement is dealt with in more detail by art.45 TFEU. It states:

"1. Freedom of movement for workers shall be secured within the Union.
2. Such freedom of movement shall entail the abolition of any discrimination based on nationality between workers of the Member States as regards employment, remuneration and other conditions of work and employment.
3. It shall entail the right, subject to limitations justified on grounds of public policy, public security or public health:
   (a) to accept offers of employment actually made;
   (b) to move freely within the territory of Member States for this purpose;
   (c) to stay in a Member State for the purpose of employment in accordance with the provisions governing the employment of nationals of that State laid down by law, regulation or administrative action;
   (d) to remain in the territory of a Member State after having been employed in that State, subject to conditions which shall be embodied in regulations to be drawn up by the Commission.
4. The provisions of this Article shall not apply to employment in the public service."

The main EU Directives and Regulations giving effect to the right to free movement of workers are:

- Regulation No. 492/2011 on freedom of movement for workers within the Union; and
- Directive 2004/38 on the right of EU citizens and their family members to move and reside freely within the territory of the Member States. (This Directive is analysed in detail in Ch.10—EU Citizenship.)

The Free Movement of Workers

The word "worker" may have very different definitions in the laws of the various Member States. The CJEU held in *Hoekstra (née Unger) v Bestuur der Bedrijfsvereniging voor Detailhandel en Ambachten* (C-75/63) that the definition of "worker" is a matter of EU law, not national law. This is to ensure the uniform application of EU law and to ensure that workers are treated in the same way in every Member State. In *Levin v Staatsecretaris va Justitie* (C-53/81), it was held that this freedom applied to part-time workers and that the rules only guaranteed free movement for workers who pursue "genuine and effective economic activity". In *Deborah Lawrie-Blum v Land Baden-Württemberg* (C-66/85), the Court held:

> "The essential feature of an employment relationship, however, is that for a certain period of time a person performs services for and under the direction of another person in return for which he receives remuneration."

It was held in *Van Duyn v Home Office* (C-41/74) that this right is directly effective. There, a Dutch woman was refused an entry permit because she was moving to work for the Scientologists, who the British government had believed to be "socially harmful". The Court held that this right has both a horizontal and a vertical direct effect.

The CJEU held in *Walrave and Koch v Association Union Cycliste Internationale* (C-36/74) that art.45 applies even where the work was done outside the EU, so long as the legal relationship of employment was entered into within the EU. It also held that EU law could apply to sport but only so far as it was an economic activity. EU law does not affect national teams because they have nothing to do with economic activity. The CJEU then explained that EU law applies to public authorities and to the rules of private associations and any other type of rules aimed at regulating employment and services. The CJEU also explained that the prohibition of discrimination based on nationality applied to all legal relationships which could be located within the territory of the Community. In *Bosman*, it held that transfer rules directly affected players' access to the employment market in other Member States and were thus capable of impeding the free movement of workers. There it was held that if free movement is indistinctly applied, it could be justified if:

1. The measures used were in pursuit of a legitimate aim; and
2. That aim was justified by pressing reasons of public interest.

Indistinctly applicable restrictions are restrictions which apply against foreign nationals and citizens of the state but are harder for foreign nationals to satisfy. These are discussed in more detail in Ch.13—Free Movement of Goods.

In *Angonese* (C-281/98), it was held that art.45 is capable of being invoked against an employer who refuses to employ someone on the grounds of nationality.

Purpose of Work

It was first held in *Levin* that the right of free movement applies regardless of why the worker takes up employment abroad. It was also held in *Levin* that a wage is required for an activity to be considered work, but the amount is not important. The Court has held that a wage does not have to be money but can be indirect reward, such as board and lodging. In *Raulin v Minister van Onderwijs en Wetenschappen* (C-357/89), it was held that the right to free movement applies whether or not the worker needs additional financial assistance from the Member State to which they move.

In *Kempf* (C-139/85), a German music teacher in the Netherlands was refused a residence payment. He gave 12 piano lessons a week and supplemented his income with welfare payments. The Dutch government argued that these lessons could not be "genuine and effective" work if they meant a person had to rely on public funds to supplement his income. The CJEU held that where a genuine part-time worker sought to supplement his income, it was irrelevant how he did so.

In *Lair v Unistat Hannover* (C-39/86), a French woman moved to Germany and worked on a number of part-time contracts. She applied to the German government for a maintenance grant to study languages at the University of Hanover. The Court held that she was entitled to a maintenance grant as an EU Citizen who had previously pursued "genuine and effective" activity in another Member State could still be considered a worker.

In *Bettray* (C-344/87), the CJEU held that a drug rehabilitation programme, which included a job tailored to the applicant's abilities, was not an effective and genuine economic activity if it was a means of rehabilitation or reintegration into society. Here the purpose of the paid employment was to help drug addicts to recover their ability to take up normal work.

This was distinguished in *Trojani* (C-465/02). In this case, a French drug addict lived in a Salvation Army hostel in Belgium. He got board, lodging and pocket money for doing jobs for 30 hours a week, as part of a "personal socio-occupational reintegration programme". He applied for a subsistence allowance from the Belgian authorities. Social reintegration was the main purpose of his employment but the Court of Justice left it to the national court to decide whether or not the employment was genuine or if they were "merely marginal and ancillary activity".

In *Brown v Secretary of State for Scotland* (C-197/86), a French student who worked in preuniversity training in Scotland claimed that he was a worker so that he could claim a maintenance grant. The CJEU held that he was a worker but, due to the ancillary purpose of his employment, he was not entitled to all the advantages available to a worker including the maintenance grant. In the subsequent case of *Bidar v London Borough of Ealing* (C-209/03), the CJEU changed its views on maintenance grants. As a result, it is unclear whether *Brown* is still good law.

Access to Social Assistance

EU citizens do not always come into employment as soon as they travel to another EU Member State in search of work. In some cases, EU citizens have the right to receive social assistance from Member States to which they have travelled. In *R. v Immigration Appeal Tribunal, Ex p. Antoniessen* (C-292/89), it was held that jobseekers do have rights pursuant to art.45 but that they do not have the full status of "worker". This restriction was designed to prevent welfare tourism. Welfare tourism is the fear that nationals from poorer Member States may travel to richer Member States, not to work, but to benefit from their more generous social welfare systems. In *Lebon* (C-316/85), it was held that social and tax advantages guaranteed to workers are not available to jobseekers.

In *D'Hoop v Office Nationale de L'Emploi* (C-224/98), the CJEU held that a Belgian who was refused an allowance because her secondary education was from France was found to have been discriminated against. There it was held:

> "A citizen of the Union must be granted in all Member States the same treatment in law as that accorded to the nationals of those Member States who find themselves in the same situation, it would be incompatible with the right of freedom of movement were a citizen, in the Member State of which he is a national, to receive treatment less favourable than he would enjoy if he had not availed himself of the opportunities offered by the Treaty in relation to freedom of movement."

In *Collins v Secretary of State for Work and Pensions* (C-138/02), the Court of Justice revisited earlier case law on free movement, as EU citizenship rights had then been introduced. Mr Collins was an Irish citizen claiming jobseekers allowance in the UK, but this was refused as he was not habitually resident in the UK. The Court of Justice held that jobseekers are now entitled to equal treatment in the host Member State. It is up to the Member State to ensure there is a genuine link between the jobseeker and the labour market and to show that indirect discrimination is justified. The Court found that he was entitled to this benefit. This approach was confirmed in *Ioanaddis* (C-258/04) and *Vatsouras* (C-22–23/08). Workers also have the same right as nationals to housing benefit and to join trade unions.

A recent case which discusses welfare tourism is *Dano v Jobcenter Leipzig* (C-333/13). There Ms Dano and her son Florin took a case when they were refused benefits by the German authorities. Ms Dano, who was born in 1989, and her son Florin, who was born in 2009, are both Romanian nationals. She had been issued a residence certificate of unlimited duration for EU nationals. They lived with her sister who provided for them. Ms Dano received child benefit for her son. She could speak German but had difficulty reading and writing it. She had not been trained in a profession and had not worked in Germany or Romania. Although her ability to work was not in dispute, there was nothing to indicate that she had ever looked for a job. The Court held:

> "Article 24(1) of Directive 2004/38 provides that all Union citizens residing on the basis of the directive in the territory of the host Member State are to enjoy equal treatment with the nationals of that Member State within the scope of the Treaty. [As a result,] a Union citizen can claim equal treatment with nationals of the host Member State [when it comes to access to social benefits, but] only if his residence in the territory of the host Member State complies with the conditions of [the] Directive."

The Court noted in the case of residence of up to three months, the right of residence is retained as long as the citizen and their family members do not become an unreasonable burden on the social assistance system of the host Member State. The host Member State is not obliged to give them social benefits during these three months. The Court also noted that for periods of residence longer than three months, the right of residence is retained only if the European Union citizen and his or her family members satisfy the conditions set out in art.7(1) of Directive 2004/38, which are that they must have sufficient resources not to become an unreasonable burden on the social assistance system of the host Member State and have comprehensive sickness insurance.

The Court found that art.7(1)(b) of the Citizenship Directive seeks to prevent economically inactive European Union citizens from using the host Member State's welfare system to fund their subsistence. Member States must have the possibility of refusing to grant social benefits to economically inactive European Union citizens who travel solely in order to obtain another Member State's social assistance where they do not have sufficient resources to claim a right of residence. To deny this would result in persons who do not have sufficient resources to provide for themselves automatically receiving social benefits upon arrival in the state. Therefore, the financial situation of each person concerned should be examined specifically, without taking account of the social benefits claimed, in order to determine whether he or she meets the condition of having sufficient resources to qualify for a right of residence under art.7(1)(b) of Directive 2004/38. The Court also tied in the right to freedom of movement with the right to freedom from discrimination found in art.18 TFEU.

The Court found that Ms Dano had been residing in Germany for more than three months, that she was not seeking employment and that she did not enter Germany in order to work. She therefore did not fall within the scope of the Citizenship Directive and was refused the benefits.

In *Alimanovic* (C-67/14), however, the Court confirmed its finding in *Dano* that in relation to access to social benefits, a European Union citizen can claim equal treatment only if his or her residence in the host Member State complies with the conditions of the Citizenship Directive. The Court found that an individual assessment of means is not required.

Access to Vocational Training

In *Gravier v City of Liege* (C-293/83), a French woman was charged a fee to enrol in a cartooning course in the prestigious Académie Royale des Beaux-Arts in the City of Liege in Belgium. This fee was not charged to Belgian nationals. Her study visa was revoked after she refused to pay. She argued that the fee was contrary to the principle of non-discrimination. There vocational training was defined as follows:

> "Any form of education which prepares for a qualification for a particular profession, trade or employment or which provides the necessary training and skills for such a profession, trade or employment is vocational training, whatever the age and the level of training of the pupils or students, and even if the training program includes an element of general education."

The Court struck down the fee, holding that access to training comes under the Treaty provisions as access to training is likely to promote free movement. That case was then followed by *Blaizot* (C-24/86). Mr Blaizot and other French students who studied at Belgian universities wanted their enrolment fee refunded after the decision in *Gravier*. The Belgian government had created a law after *Gravier* that excluded claims for refunds, except only for those who had started seeking a refund before the courts before the *Gravier* decision was given. It was held that the university studies were vocational training and that the imposition of fees was discriminatory.

In *Kranemann* (C-109/04), a German trainee lawyer in London wanted to be reimbursed for travel expenses from Germany. He was being educated in Germany but did part of his training in London. The CJEU found that legal trainees carry out "genuine and effective activity as an employed person" and are therefore workers for the purposes of art.45.

Brown and *Lair* appear to show that only access to training is protected and not additional matters such as registration fees. In *Commission v Austria* (C-147/03), it was held that Member States cannot plead the homogeneity of the higher education system to justify discrimination.

Workers' Families

The principle of non-discrimination has been extended to a migrant worker's family as, otherwise, the right to freedom of movement would not be worth very much because people would not want to leave their families. The rights of families comes from the workers' right of free movement. Workers' families have the right to travel with them to another Member State under art.2 of the Citizenship Directive. There was previously quite a lot of case law on this area; however, it has mostly been taken over by the EU secondary legislation.

Article 10 of Regulation 492/2011 provides for equal access for the children of a resident worker to the host Member State's educational courses. It states:

> "The children of a national of a Member State who is or has been employed in the territory of another Member State shall be admitted to that State's general educational, apprenticeship and vocational training courses under the same conditions as the nationals of that State, if such children are residing in its territory."

Article 13 of the Citizenship Directive covers the right to retain residence in the event of divorces and annulments etc. and art.12(3) provides:

> "The Union citizen's departure from the host Member State or his/her death shall not entail loss of the right of residence of his/her children or of the parent who has actual custody of the children, irrespective of nationality, if the children reside in the host Member State and are enrolled at an educational establishment, for the purpose of studying there, until the completion of their studies."

In *Singh v The Minister for Justice* (C-218/14), the marriage between an EU citizen and a non-citizen ended after the EU citizen left the EU Member State. The Court ruled that, in principle, third-country national family members of an EU citizen who has moved out of a Member State lose their right to reside in that state under the Citizenship Directive as soon as the EU citizen moves out. It is, however, open to a Member State to be more generous if it wishes to be, as Ireland was in this situation.

The death of the EU citizen will not deprive their family members of the right to remain in the country. If it had not already been acquired, they will do so if:

1. They resided continuously in the state for two years prior to the worker's death;
2. The worker died from an occupational disease or accident; or
3. The surviving spouse was a national of that state and lost nationality on marriage to the deceased.

Obstacles to Access to Employment

The Court of Justice has found that measures which impede the free movement of workers may violate art.45 even where they do not discriminate on the ground of nationality. Any obstacle, discriminatory or otherwise, which restricts the entry, residence and access to employment of a migrant worker in a Member State will breach art.45. In particular, they will breach art.45 if they constitute an excessive obstacle to the free movement of workers.

Direct and Indirect Discrimination

Article 45 TFEU prohibits direct and indirect discrimination. In *Sotgiu v Deutsch Bundespost* (C-152/73), it was held that the rules on equality forbid

> "not only overt discrimination by reason of nationality but also all covert forms of discrimination which, by the application of other criteria of differentiation, lead in fact to the same result."

An example of indirect discrimination is *Ugliola* (C-15/69). In this case, a German law said that time spent in military service could be taken into account when calculating an employee's pension benefits. This applied to those who had done their military service in the German Army regardless of nationality. Mr Ugliola was an Italian living in Germany and was unable to benefit from this as he had done his military service in the Italian army. This law was indirectly discriminatory; even though it applied equally to people of all nationalities, it was more likely that Germans would have done military service in the German Army than people from other Member States. Accordingly, the CJEU struck it down.

In *Flynn v Adjudication Officer* (C-237/94), an Irishman working in the UK applied for a grant to cover his son's funeral expenses. It was refused as his son was being buried in Ireland, not in the UK. The Court of Justice held that it was more likely that non-nationals would have their relatives buried outside the UK and this refusal was therefore indirectly discriminatory.

Giersch (C-20/12) dealt with residence-based restrictions on financial aid for students. According to Luxembourg law, students received financial aid if they were residents in Luxembourg, regardless of nationality. The measure was challenged on the basis of Regulation No. 492/2011, which requires equal treatment in relation to social advantages. The Court found the residence requirement to be indirectly discriminatory. However, it accepted that "increasing the proportion of residents with a higher education degree in order to promote the development of the economy" was a legitimate objective which could justify differential treatment, and that a residence requirement could be appropriate to achieve that goal.

Public Service Exception

According to art.45(3) TFEU, the right to free movement is subject to limitations "justified on grounds of public policy, public security or public health". These exceptions also apply to the freedom of establishment and free movement of services and is analysed in Ch.12. Article 45(4) states: "The provisions of this article shall not apply to employment in the public service." In *Sotgiu v Deutsch Bundespost* (C-152/73), it was held that "public service" is to be determined by the CJEU and not by the Member States. Again, this is to ensure the uniform and consistent application of EU law throughout the Member States, as different Member States may have different views on what constitutes public service. In *Commission v Belgium* (C-149/79), it was held that public service involves

> "a series of posts which involve direct or indirect participation in the exercise of powers conferred by public law and duties designed to safeguard the general interests of the state or of other public authorities. Such posts in fact presume on the part of those occupying them the existence of a special relationship of allegiance to the state and reciprocity of rights and duties which form the foundation of the bond of nationality."

Certain jobs with Belgian local authorities and public undertakings were reserved for Belgian nationals under this exception regardless of the nature of the work that was to be done. This included jobs such as nurses, night watchmen and unskilled railway workers. It was found that the activities cannot be brought under this exception by the state by including them within the scope of the state's public law and taking responsibility for their performance. It was held that these jobs did not fall under the public service exception, bar a few exceptions.

In *Commission v Italy* (C-225/85), Italy claimed that laws which protected the security and tenure of Italians but not non-Italians at the National Research Centre (CNR) came under this exception. They claimed that it was financed by public funds and satisfied the general interests of the Member State. The Court of Justice decided as follows:

> "Simply referring to the general tasks of the CNR and listing the duties of all its researchers is not sufficient to establish that the researchers are responsible for exercising powers conferred by public law or for safeguarding the general interests of the State. Only the duties of management or of advising the State on scientific and technical questions could be described as employment in the public service within the meaning of Article 48(4). However, it has not been established that those duties were carried out by CNR researchers."

In *Colegio de Oficiales de law Marina Mercante Espanola* (C-405/01), the posts of master and chief mate of a ship were reserved for Spaniards on board merchant ships flying a Spanish flag because they had police powers in the event of an emergency. It was found that the public service exception could only be used if public law powers were exercised on a regular basis, not where it is merely a minor part of the job.

12 Freedom of Establishment and Free Movement of Services and Capital

Introduction

The freedom of establishment and the free movement of services are two very closely intertwined freedoms; it can sometimes be difficult to see where one begins and the other ends. They are often mentioned in the same Treaty articles. For example, art.15(2) of the EU Charter of Fundamental Rights provides that "[e]very citizen of the Union has the freedom to seek employment, to work, to exercise right of establishment and to provide services in any Member State", and art.56(1) TFEU states

> "restrictions on freedom to provide services within the Union shall be prohibited in respect of nationals of Member States who are established in a Member State other than that of the person for whom the services are intended."

These freedoms share the same exceptions and there is cross-over here with the free movement of persons. This chapter will analyse these freedoms and will also look at the free movement of capital, another of the four freedoms guaranteed by the internal market. It deals with the movement of money and payments. These topics are important; for example, services account for between 60 and 70 per cent of GDP in the EU, and, as this chapter will show, they are deeply connected with one another.

Freedom of Establishment

The freedom of establishment is the right which allows citizens to practise a profession instead of just working for someone else. Establishment was defined in *R. v Secretary of State for Transport, Ex p. Factortame Ltd* (C-221/89) as:

> "The actual pursuit of an economic activity through a fixed establishment in another Member State for an indefinite period."

Establishment also includes the right to be self-employed or to set up and manage firms and companies. The freedom of establishment is protected by arts 49–55 TFEU. Article 49 states:

> "Within the framework of the provisions set out below, restrictions on the freedom of establishment of nationals of a Member State in the territory of another Member State shall be prohibited. Such prohibition shall also apply to restrictions on the setting-up of agencies, branches or subsidiaries by nationals of any Member State established in the territory of any Member State.
>
> Freedom of establishment shall include the right to take up and pursue activities as self-employed persons and to set up and manage undertakings, in particular companies or firms within the meaning of the second paragraph of Article 54, under the conditions laid down for its own nationals by the law of the country where such establishment is effected, subject to the provisions of the Chapter relating to capital."

Freedom of establishment does not just apply to individuals but it also applies to corporate bodies and companies. Under art.54 TFEU, they are treated as being like individuals. The right of EU citizens to be self-employed includes the right to enter and to reside in the Member State where they want to be self-employed. This right is extended to their family members.

The Court of Justice in *Commission v The Netherlands* (C-299/02) held:

> "It is settled case-law that Article 49 precludes any national measure which, even though it is applicable without discrimination on grounds of nationality, is liable to hamper or to render less attractive the exercise by Community nationals of the freedom of establishment."

This applies even where there is no discrimination on the grounds of nationality. The Court noted that this can be restricted on the grounds of public policy, public security and public health or by pressing reasons of general interest.

In *Van Binsbergen* (C-33/74), Advocate General Mayras gave an opinion stating that equality of treatment by reason of nationality equally underlies the Treaty provisions on establishment, services and workers. This is because they demand equal treatment for people who have used their right to freedom of movement and settled in another Member State. This means the case law examined in relation to the free movement of workers will be relevant here.

The same prohibition on direct or indirect discrimination that applies to the freedom of movement of workers also applies to the freedom of establishment.

Case Law on Establishment

In *Reyners v Belgium* (C-2/74), a Dutchman was refused admission to the Belgian bar because he was not a Belgian. This meant he could not practise in Belgium as a lawyer. It was found that this difference in treatment between Belgians and foreigners was an infringement of his right to establishment. The Court came to similar conclusions in the cases of a Belgian lawyer and a British architect in France (*Thieffry v Conseil de l'Ordre des Avocats à la Cour de Paris* (C-71/76) and *Patrick v Ministère des Affaires Culturelles* (C-11/77)), and a Dutch motor insurance claims investigator in Italy (*Van Ameyde v UCI* (C-90/76)). In *Klopp* (C-107/83), it was held that it is possible to be established in more than one country at the same time.

In *International Transport Workers Federation v Viking Line* (C-438/05), it was held that art.49 on the freedom of establishment could be used directly by employers against trade unions seeking to take collective action in furtherance of a trade dispute.

Article 49 gives individuals the right to leave their home state without restriction. While companies are generally treated as being the same as humans when it comes to establishment, the law here is different. In *R. (Daily Mail and General Trust plc) v HM Treasury* (C-81/87), it was held that it was not an infringement of art.49 where a Member State restricted a company moving out of a country. This meant the Daily Mail newspaper could not evade tax by moving to Holland without first settling its tax bill in the UK. This was affirmed in *Cartesio* (C-210/06).

In *Young v The Pharmaceutical Society* [1995] 2 I.R. 91 and *Scally v Minister for the Environment* [1996] 1 I.R. 367, there were failed attempts to rely on the direct effect of the right of establishment in Ireland.

The Freedom to Provide Services

EU citizens also have the freedom to provide services in other EU Member States. This can happen in a number of different ways. The person providing the service can go to the other Member State and provide it or the person receiving the service can travel to the person providing it. In some cases, both nationals can stay in their home state and the service can be provided through the internet or broadcasting or some other means. *Luisi and Carbone v Ministerio del Tesoro* (C-26/83) says that the free movement of services includes the right to travel to receive services as well as to provide them.

As we have seen, the freedom to provide services is linked to the freedom of establishment and both freedoms involve professional activities for profit. Established professionals often provide a service; in some cases, it might be difficult to tell if someone is established in a host state or simply providing services there. This can happen in cases where the provision of services takes a long time. The difference between establishment and providing services is that the right of establishment involves permanent installation in a Member State in order to pursue an economic activity there, whereas providing services does not require a place of business within the state. Establishment is more permanent than providing services (see *Gebhard* (C-55/94), discussed below).

The freedom to provide services overlaps with other freedoms; for example, someone involved in the distribution of goods may arguably be providing goods and services. The Court of Justice will normally try to examine a free movement claim under one freedom only. They will do this by examining which of the freedoms the case is predominantly related to. The Court of Justice in *Fidium Finanz* (C-452/04) held that there is no particular order of priority between the fundamental freedoms. If the Court cannot examine the case under the law of one heading, it will analyse the case under both headings.

Articles 57–62 TFEU

The free movement of services by EU nationals is found in art.56 TFEU, with further guidance in arts 57–62 TFEU. This freedom promotes the free circulation of services within the Member States. Article 57 TFEU gives the definition of services:

> "Services shall be considered to be 'services' within the meaning of the Treaties where they are normally provided for remuneration, in so far as they are not governed by the provisions relating to freedom of movement for goods, capital and persons.
>
> 'Services' shall in particular include:
>
> a) activities of an industrial character;
> b) activities of a commercial character;
> c) activities of craftsmen;
> d) activities of the professions."

Article 57 further states:

> "Without prejudice to the provisions of the Chapter relating to the right of establishment, the person providing a service may, in order to do so, temporarily pursue his activity in the Member State where the service is provided, under the same conditions as are imposed by that State on its own nationals."

While services make up a large percentage of the EU's GDP, legislation in the area is not as developed as in other areas. This has been addressed by the Directive on Services in the Internal Market (Directive 2006/123/EC) which aims to help make the EU "the world's most dynamic and competitive economy" by removing barriers to the free movement of services and freedom of establishment. In 2011, activities within the scope of this Directive made up almost half of the EU's GDP.

The Court of Justice has no moral agenda when it comes to services. In *Jany* (C-268/99), prostitutes were found to be providing services. In *SPUC v Grogan* (C-159/90), the provision of abortions was found to be a service. These may be areas where it is an objectively justified discrimination where a Member State refuses to allow them. In *Sager v Dennemeyer* (C-159/90), it was held that the provision of services may be justifiably limited on the grounds of the public interest. In *Coffeeshop Siberie* (C-158/98) and *Verninging Happy Family Rustenburgerstraat* (C-289/86), it was held that this right did not apply to tourists who were exercising their freedom of movement rights in order to purchase cannabis, which was illegal in their home countries.

Gebhard

In *Gebhard* (C-55/94), the Court tried to draw together the case law on the four freedoms. This was about a German who was qualified as a German lawyer but who claimed in Italy that he was qualified as an Italian lawyer. He gave legal advice and assistance to Italian speakers in Germany and to German speakers in Italy. The Milanese Bar took a case against him for claiming to be an Italian lawyer and this was referred to the CJEU. There it was held that:

> "The concept of establishment within the meaning of the Treaty is therefore a very broad one, allowing a Community national to participate, on a stable and continuous basis, in the economic life of a Member State other than his State of origin and to profit therefrom, so contributing to economic and social interpenetration within the

Community in the sphere of activities as self-employed persons (see, to this effect, Case 2/74 *Reyners v Belgium*).

In contrast, where the provider of services moves to another Member State, the provisions of the chapter on services, in particular the third paragraph of Article 60, envisage that he is to pursue his activity there on a temporary basis.

As the Advocate General has pointed out, the temporary nature of the activities in question has to be determined in the light, not only of the duration of the provision of the service, but also of its regularity, periodicity or continuity. The fact that the provision of services is temporary does not mean that the provider of services within the meaning of the Treaty may not equip himself with some form of infrastructure in the host Member State (including an office, chambers or consulting rooms) in so far as such infrastructure is necessary for the purposes of performing the services in question."

Exceptions

There are a number of shared exceptions to the freedom of establishment and the freedom to provide services. The "Official Authority" exception is found in art.51 TFEU and the public policy security and health exceptions can be found in art.52 TFEU.

Official Authority

Article 51 TFEU provides for an exception where activities are concerned with the exercise of "Official Authority". This exception means that jobs which are connected with the official authority of the Member State can be reserved for people from that Member State. This is similar to the public service exception found under art.45(4) TFEU which applies to the free movement of workers. Article 51 states:

> "The provisions of this Chapter shall not apply, so far as any given Member State is concerned, to activities which in that State are connected, even occasionally, with the exercise of official authority.
>
> The European Parliament and the Council, acting in accordance with the ordinary legislative procedure, may rule that the provisions of this Chapter shall not apply to certain activities."

The official authority exception was given a narrow interpretation in *Reyners*. In that case, the issue was whether lawyers as a profession would fall under this exception because some of their activities are connected to the official authority of the state or if it was only those specific activities which would fall under the exception. The Court held:

> "Having regard to the fundamental character of freedom of establishment and the rule on equal treatment with nationals in the system of the Treaty, the exceptions allowed by the first paragraph of Article 51 TFEU cannot be given a scope which should exceed the objective for which this exemption clause was inserted.
>
> The first paragraph of Article 51 TFEU must enable Member States to exclude non-nationals from taking up functions involving the exercise of official authority which are connected with the activities of the self-employed person provided for in Article 49 TFEU.
>
> This need is fully satisfied when the exclusion of nationals is limited to those activities which taken on their own constitute a direct and specific connection with the exercise of official authority.
>
> An extension of the exception allowed by Article 55 to a whole profession would be possible only in cases where such activities were linked with that profession in such a way that freedom of establishment would result in imposing on the Member State concerned the obligation to allow the exercise, even occasionally, by non-nationals of functions appertaining to official authority.
>
> This extension is on the other hand not possible when, within the framework of an independent profession, the activities connected with the exercise of official authority are separable from the professional activity in question taken as a whole."

It can be seen from this that this exception is very limited. It is restricted to activities which constitute a "direct and specific connection" with the exercise of official authority. The Court added that this exception should only apply to an entire profession in exceptional circumstances and that it could not apply to an independent profession where the activities connected with the exercise of official authority could be separated from the profession's activities as a whole.

There have been many unsuccessful attempts by states seeking to rely on this exception. These cases include teachers (*Commission v Greece* (C-147/86)); programming and computer systems for public administration (*Commission v Italy* (C-3/88)); experts' reports on traffic accidents (*Commission v Greece* (C-306/89)); public lotteries (*Commission v Italy* (C-272/91)); internal auditors (*Thijssen* (C-42/92)); security staff (*Commission v Spain* (C-114/97)); notaries (*Commission v Germany* (C-54/08)); and, in

Penarraoja Fa (C-372/09), it was held that the court translators did not come within this exception either.

PUBLIC POLICY HEALTH AND SECURITY

Article 52 TFEU provides for exceptions on the grounds of public policy health and security. These exceptions have also been narrowly interpreted by the CJEU. Similar exceptions exist for the free movement of workers under art.45(3) TFEU. Article 27 of Directive 2004/38 (the Citizenship Directive) covers these exceptions when they apply to natural persons. There is some cross-over here between free movement of persons and free movement of services and establishment. Measures taken on the grounds of art.27 must comply with proportionality and be based on the personal conduct of the person concerned. The burden of proof is on the state to show the rule is justified (*Commission v Italy* (260/04)).

In *Van Duyn* (C-41/74), the fact that the British government considered the scientologists to be socially harmful was not enough to stop someone entering the country to work for them. In *Adoui and Cornuaille v Belgium* (C-115 and 116/81), two French prostitutes were refused residence permits in Belgium. The Court held that Member States could not deny residence to non-nationals because of conduct which would not give rise to repressive measures against their own nationals. However, in *Ministre de l'Intérieur v Olazabal* (C-100/01), a case which dealt with the free movement of workers rather than services or establishment, France relied on the public security exception when it banned a Basque separatist from living in France due to his activities with ETA. The Court of Justice here held that the exceptions allow Member States to adopt measures against nationals of other Member States which they could not apply to their own nationals on public policy grounds. In *Jan Anfinn Wahl v The Icelandic State* (E-15/12), the EFTA court held that Iceland did not have to declare the Hells Angels unlawful before it could deny a Hells Angel the right to enter. In *Calfa* (C-348/96), it was held that a person could be expelled from a country for a criminal offence if their conduct creates a genuine and sufficiently serious threat to the fundamental interests of society. However, where the expulsion was automatic without regard to personal conduct, this would not be allowed.

When it comes to public health, only serious infectious diseases can justify this restriction. Diseases which occur three months after the date of arrival are not grounds for expulsion.

In joined cases *Vicoplus* (C-307–309/09), the Court of Justice ruled that the freedom to provide services, read in connection with the Act of Accession 2003, was not a bar to the Dutch policy of requiring work permits for Polish workers during the transitional period provided in the Act.

There is a lengthy discussion of these exceptions in *Van Binsbergen*; there, the Court held:

> "[T]aking into account the particular nature of the services to be provided, specific requirements imposed on the person providing the service cannot be considered incompatible with the Treaty where they have as their purpose the application of professional rules justified by the general good—in particular rules relating to organization, qualifications, professional ethics, supervision and liability—which are binding upon any person established in the state in which the service is provided, where the person providing the service would escape from the ambit of those rules being established in another Member State.
>
> Likewise, a Member State cannot be denied the right to take measures to prevent the exercise by a person providing services whose activity is entirely or principally directed towards its territory of the freedom guaranteed by Article 59 for the purpose of avoiding the professional rules of conduct which would be applicable to him if he were established within that state; such a situation may be subject to judicial control under the provisions of the chapter relating to the right of establishment and not of that on the provision of services.
>
> In accordance with these principles, the requirement that persons whose functions are to assist the administration of justice must be permanently established for professional purposes within the jurisdiction of certain courts or tribunals cannot be considered incompatible with the provisions of Articles 59 and 60, where such requirement is objectively justified by the need to ensure observance of professional rules of conduct connected, in particular, with the administration of justice and with respect for professional ethics.
>
> That cannot, however, be the case when the provision of certain services in a Member State is not subject to any sort of qualification or professional regulation and when the requirement of habitual residence is fixed by reference to the territory of the state in question.
>
> In relation to a professional activity the exercise of which is similarly unrestricted within the territory of a particular Member State, the requirement of residence within that state constitutes a restriction which is incompatible with Articles 59 and 60 of the treaty if the administration of justice can satisfactorily be ensured by measures which are less restrictive, such as the choosing of an address for service."

The Court has also held that restrictive measures must respect fundamental rights (see *Ellinimki Radiophonia Tileorassi* (C-260/89), *Familia press* (C-368/95) and *Carpenter v Home Secretary* (C-60/00)). In *Omega* (C-36/02), the public policy grounds were successfully invoked to prevent a service in Germany. Here Lazertag was banned because it involved "playing at killing"; this was found to respect fundamental rights and was upheld. In *Mac Quen* (C-108/96), a Belgian law which said that only ophthalmologists could provide eye examinations was upheld on health grounds, even though it prevented opticians from providing this service.

Free Movement of Capital

The free movement of capital was one of the four freedoms and was in the original Treaty of Rome. It is intended to promote movement of investments such as shares and property purchases. Free movement of capital is about making economic sectors accessible to people who work in financial markets, allowing them to buy, sell and invest. The free movement of capital is unique amongst the freedoms as it applies equally worldwide, including to non-Member States. Originally the provisions on this freedom were weaker than those relating to the other freedoms; however, this changed when it was overhauled by the Maastricht Treaty in 1994. This may be why it has the least amount of case law of the four freedoms. The Treaty of Maastricht made economic and monetary union an objective, first by completing the internal market (which guarantees the four freedoms) and then by introducing the euro.

The free movement of capital and payments is governed by arts 63–66 TFEU. The general principle is given by art.63:

> "1. Within the framework of the provisions set out in this Chapter, all restrictions on the movement of capital between Member States and between Member States and third countries shall be prohibited.
>
> 2. Within the framework of the provisions set out in this Chapter, all restrictions on payments between Member States and between Member States and third countries shall be prohibited."

This was held to have direct effect in *Sanz de Lera* (C-163/94, C-165/94 and C-250/94). The Treaty provisions do not define movement of capital, but the CJEU held in *Trummer and Mayer* (C-222/97) that reference can be made to a non-exhaustive list found in Directive 88/361. It is for the CJEU to decide, with the aid of this Directive, whether a measure is a restriction on the movement of capital. Examples might include measures taken by Member States to dissuade its citizens from acquiring capital in other Member States (*Sandoz* (C-439/47)).

In *Commission v Germany* (C-112/05) and in joined cases *Federconsumatori* (C-463/04 and 464/04), it was held that national measures must be regarded as restrictions under art.63(1) TFEU if they are liable to prevent or limit the acquisition of stakes in undertakings or to deter investors from other Member States from investing their capital.

In *Commission v Italy* (C-531/06), the Commission complained that Italian legislation:

A) Restricted pharmacists from holding significant stakes in companies or firms operating pharmacies, which would give them a definite influence over the companies' decisions, and this, therefore, impinged on the freedom of establishment.
B) Discouraged investors from other Member States who were not pharmacists from acquiring smaller stakes in those companies or firms which did not confer this amount of influence, which impinged on the free movement of capital.

The Court examined the legislation in light of freedom of establishment under art.49 and free movement of capital under art.63. It found that the restrictions on freedom of establishment and free movement of capital applied without discrimination on grounds of nationality and could be justified by overriding reasons in the general interest once the restrictions were proportionate. Here the Court found that the restrictions were justified on the grounds of protection of health.

Exceptions

There are a number of exceptions to art.63 which can be found within the Treaty and within the case law of the CJEU. These exceptions can be found in arts 64–66 TFEU, as well as arts 75 and 143–144 TFEU. Others have developed through case law.

Article 64 allows Member States to continue to apply restrictions to third countries in respect of direct investment which existed on a certain date.

Article 65(1) TFEU allows for different tax treatment of non-residents and foreign investment, although this must not represent a means of arbitrary discrimination or a distinguished restriction per art.65(3) TFEU.

Article 65(1b) TFEU and art.52(1) allows Member States to apply restrictions for public policy or public security reasons and allows Member States "to take all requisite measures to prevent infringements of national law and regulations".

Article 66 TFEU allows for restrictions regarding third countries to safeguard against serious difficulties for the operation of economic and monetary union.

Article 75 TFEU provides for the possibility of financial sanctions against individuals, groups or non-state entities to prevent and combat terrorism.

Articles 143 and 144 TFEU allow for the taking of protective balance of payments measures, where difficulties jeopardise the functioning of the internal market or where a sudden crisis occurs.

The Court of Justice in joined cases *Commission v The Netherlands* (C-282/04 and C-283/04) held that the overriding general interest can be an exception to the free movement of capital. There, it was held

> "that the guarantee of a service of general interest, such as universal postal service, may constitute an overriding reason in the general interest capable of justifying an obstacle to the free movement of capital."

In *Commission v Italy* (C-174/04), the Court held that the use of this exception must be proportionate. Similarly, in *Albore* (C-423/98), the Court held that the use of the Treaty exceptions must be proportionate. The Court of Justice in *Église de Scientologie* (C-54/99) decided that the difficulty in identifying and blocking capital once it has entered a Member State may, in principle, justify differential treatment of transactions involving foreign direct investment.

13 Free Movement of Goods

Introduction

The free movement of goods is arguably the most important of the four freedoms guaranteed by the EU. If a product is manufactured in Ireland, it should be able to be sold in any other EU Member State on the same basis as goods from any other Member State. Goods from outside the EU enjoy free movement once they enter the EU. The EU internal market (also known as the single market and previously known as the common market) is the means by which the freedoms are guaranteed. Articles 2 and 3 of the Treaty of Rome provided that the purpose of the Treaty was to establish a customs union or common market, and generally to foster closer relations and increase trade amongst Member States.

This freedom is widely regarded as being one of the biggest EU success stories and was one of the largest attractions to Ireland when it joined in 1972. It allows EU producers to sell their goods throughout one of the largest trading blocks in the world and EU consumers to select the cheapest and best products from a large market. Almost three quarters of trade in the EU is in goods. This is one of the largest areas of EU law and has generated a lot of case law. This right is protected by arts 26, 38 and 37 TFEU. In analysing this topic, we will look at the free movement of goods, customs duties and internal taxation, quantitative restrictions, as well as the limits and exceptions.

What are Goods?

The most obvious question when dealing with the free movement of goods is "what is a good?", as the word "goods" can cover a lot. Articles 34 and 35 TFEU cover all types of imports and exports of goods and products. Any product with an economic value can be a good.

Goods were defined by the CJEU in *Commission v Italy* (C-7/68) (the Italian Art Treasures case). In this case, the Italian Government prohibited the exportation of art treasures and claimed that they were not "goods". Italy wanted to protect its long artistic history which stretches through the renaissance back to the Romans. A catalogue was made of all artistic or archaeological objects, collections or monuments, including objects which belonged to private institutions, individuals and the church. Anything in the catalogue could not be sold outside of Italy. Anything not in the catalogue could be sold, but only with the permission of a government minister. The Court of Justice defined goods as being "products which can be valued in money and which are capable, as such, of forming the subject of Commercial transactions" and held that the works of art came under this definition.

One interesting case on the definition of a "good" is *Commission v Belgium* (C-2/90) (Walloon Waste). The Wallonia region in Belgium banned the importation of waste from other areas, including other EU Member States, because it faced an "abnormal large-scale inflow of waste from other regions". Waste coming from anywhere outside the region was classified as being foreign. When the case was heard, Belgium claimed that waste was not a good if it could not be recycled or reused because it has no commercial value. The Court held that waste was a good as it could be the subject of a commercial transaction and it had a certain value.

Interference with the Free Movement of Goods

The EU takes any measures which may restrict the free movement of goods very seriously and it will do all it can to prevent them. The free movement of goods can be interfered with in a number of ways by Member States in order to give their own goods an advantage over foreign goods. The most obvious way of doing this is by imposing customs duties. These duties will make foreign goods more expensive than domestic goods. This is forbidden by arts 28–30 TFEU. Another way is by imposing taxes which discriminate against imports. This is covered by arts 110–113 TFEU. A Member State may also impose quotas reducing the amount of foreign goods which can be imported. These are known as quantitative restrictions and are forbidden by arts 34–36 TFEU. Measures and charges having equivalent effect are also forbidden. These are things which are not called customs duties or quantitative restrictions but in practice they have the same effect as them.

Customs Duties and Internal Taxation and Measures Having Equivalent Effect

One of the objectives of the European Union is to establish an internal market built on a customs union. In a customs union, goods produced in one Member State should be able to move freely in all Member States without custom duties. Goods from outside the customs union should pay a common customs duty when they enter and be able to circulate freely within the union thereafter.

Article 28 TFEU states that "[t]he Union shall comprise a customs union which shall cover all trade in goods". It explains that this shall involve the prohibition between Member States of customs duties on imports and exports and of all charges having equivalent effect, and will also involve the adoption of a common customs tariff in their relations with third countries. The EU is a customs union and the EU customs union includes a number of countries outside the European Union: Monaco, Andora, San Marino and Turkey. Article 30 explains: "Customs duties on imports and exports and charges having equivalent effect shall be prohibited between Member States. This prohibition shall also apply to customs duties of a fiscal nature."

Prohibition on Customs Duties

Article 30 TFEU prohibits customs duties on imports and exports. Customs duties are taxes which are imposed when a good crosses a border. These interfere with the free movement of goods as they would discourage producers from sending their goods abroad if they have to pay tax on them and people will be discouraged from buying importing goods if they have to pay extra for them. Customs duties, no matter how small, are absolutely forbidden by the EU. The Court of Justice has made it clear that this rule depends on the effect of the duty or charge, not on its purpose. In the *Italian Art Treasures* case, Italy claimed an export tax was not to raise revenue but to protect its national treasures and its artistic, historic and archaeological history. The Court found that even though the tax was insignificant, it should be abolished.

This was followed by the joint cases *Diamantarbeiders* (C-2–3/69). There the Belgian government imposed a charge on the importation of diamonds which went to a fund for diamond workers. Belgium argued that this was for a legitimate purpose. None of the charge remained with the government, but was spent on diamond workers. The charge could not protect native production as Belgium does not produce any diamonds. The CJEU confirmed that it was the effect of the measure rather than its purpose that matters. The Court held that any charge which is imposed makes goods more expensive and less competitive. Neither the aims nor the effects of such a charge are relevant, it does not matter if the measure is discriminatory or not. This applies to customs duties and charges having equivalent effect even if it is not imposed for the benefit of the Member State, is not discriminatory or protective in effect or if the product on which the charge is imposed is not in competition with any domestic product.

Charges Having Equivalent Effect to a Customs Duty

Article 30 TFEU prohibits customs duties and charges having equivalent effect to a customs duty ("CEE"). CEE is not defined in the Treaty but in the case law. A CEE is something which, although not called a customs duty, in practise has the same effect as one. According to the case law of the CJEU, any financial charge, however small, and no matter what it is called or how it is applied, which is imposed unilaterally on goods by reason of the fact that they cross a frontier and which is not a customs duty is a charge having equivalent effect under art.30.

The CJEU defined CEE in *Commission v Italy* (C-24/68) (the Italian statistics case). Here Italy imposed a small duty on goods imported and exported from other states in order to collect statistics. The Court held the following:

> "Any pecuniary charge, however small and whatever its designation and mode of application, which is imposed unilaterally on domestic or foreign goods by reason of the fact that they cross a frontier, and which is not a customs duty in the strict sense, constitutes a charge having equivalent effect ... even if it is not imposed for the benefit of the state, is not discriminatory or protective in effect and if the product on which the charge is imposed is not in competition with any domestic product."

One case which distinguishes between customs duties and CEEs is *Bresciani v Amministrazione Italiana delle Finanze* (C-87/75). There it was held that a charge is a customs duty if it is proportionate to the value of the goods; however, if it is proportionate to the quantity, it is a CEE.

Exceptions

A charge which falls within art.30 cannot be justified; however, a charge which falls outside it may be. Charges which are allowed include charges imposed to discharge an EU law obligation imposed or to cover the cost of services rendered to the importer.

In *Bresciani*, the CJEU had to decide whether a charge imposed by Italian authorities for compulsory inspections on raw cow hides was a CEE. The Court rejected the Italian argument that the charge was proportionate to the quantity of imported goods. Article 30 TFEU prohibits any charge by reason of the fact that a good crosses a frontier. It also held that the public, rather than traders, should pay for inspections to maintain public health. Italy claimed that domestic producers were subject to similar charges. The Court held that charges could be allowed as part of the general system of internal taxation, provided they are applied according to the same criteria, at the same stage of production and in the same way to domestic and imported products. They would then fall outside art.30.

In *Commission v Germany* (C-18/87) (Re: animals inspection fees), Germany imposed charges covering the costs incurred maintaining inspection facilities. The inspections were required by European law (Directive 81/389/EC on the protection of live animals during international transport) and had the objective of promoting the free movement of goods. This was held not to be a CEE. From this it can be seen that charges made for services are not a CEE if they meet the following conditions:

1. The services are required by EU Law;
2. The charges do not exceed the actual cost of the services;
3. The services promote the free movement of goods; and
4. The services are part of a general system applied with the same criteria to domestic and imported products.

Where an inspection is permitted by EU law but is not mandatory, charges imposed to recover the costs of the inspection are prohibited (*Commission v Belgium* (314/82)).

Internal Taxes

Article 30 forbids duties when goods cross a border. This would not be much use if states could then impose discriminatory taxes on goods once they are inside the state. This is forbidden by arts 110–112 TFEU. These articles require that Member States not impose taxes on products of other Member States larger than those imposed on similar domestic products. Article 110 states:

> "No Member State shall impose, directly or indirectly, on the products of other Member States any internal taxation of any kind in excess of that imposed directly or indirectly on similar domestic products.
>
> Furthermore, no Member State shall impose on the products of other Member States any internal taxation of such a nature as to afford indirect protection to other products."

In *Commission v Italy* (C-323/87) (taxation of rum), the CJEU held that the purpose of this is to

> "ensure the free movement of goods between the Member States under normal conditions of competition, by eliminating all forms of protection which might result from the application of discriminatory internal taxation against products from other Member States, and to guarantee absolute neutrality of internal taxation as regards competition between domestic and imported products."

While customs duties and CEE are absolutely prohibited, charges which fall under art.110 are only prohibited when they are protective or discriminatory.

Discriminatory Tax Provisions

In *Bergandi v Directeur general des impôts* (C-252/86), the Court held art.110 arises whenever "a fiscal levy is likely to discourage import of goods originating in other Member States to the benefit of domestic production". Article 110(1) prohibits direct and indirect discrimination, while art.110(2) protects against discrimination against goods which are different to but still in competition with domestic law products.

Article 110(1)

Article 110(1) prohibits similar products from being taxed differently. The Court in *Commission v France* (168/78) defined similar products as those which have similar characteristics and meet the same needs from the point of view of consumers. In this case, the Court held that spirits based on grain, such as vodka, are similar to spirits based on wine and fruit, such as cognac.

In *John Walker & Sons v Ministeriet for Skatter* (C-243/84), the Court held that whiskey and fruit liquor wines are not similar as they are produced differently, have different alcoholic strengths and consumers did not view them as similar. In *Commission v Italy* (C-184/85), the Court determined that bananas are not similar to other fruit because they contain minerals. The Court held that a consumption tax of 50 per cent on the purchase price of bananas was protective where there was no similar tax on domestic fruit. In *Commission v France* (C-302/00) (tobacco), dark and light tobacco cigarettes were found to be similar. The Court noted that they were manufactured from different types of tobacco using similar processes; their tastes were similar even if they used different amounts of tobacco; they satisfied the same needs of consumers, even if dark tobacco tended to be smoked by older smokers; and EU law treated them as being the same.

Article 110(1) prohibits direct and indirect discrimination. Direct discrimination is treating an imported good worse than a domestic good because it is imported. In *Lutticke* (C-57/65), Germany imposed a tax on foreign powdered milk which did not apply to German powdered milk; this was direct discrimination. Indirect discrimination is discrimination which does not appear discriminatory but proves to be so in practice. *Humblot v Director des Services Fiscaux* (C-112/84) arose from French car tax which was indirectly discriminatory. If a car's engine capacity was above 1600cc, the car was subject to a higher tax. In practice, no French cars had an engine capacity over 1600cc, so this tax only applied to imported cars. This was found to be discriminatory.

Article 110(2)

Article 110(2) covers goods which may not be similar to domestic goods but which might still be in competition with them. In *Commission v United Kingdom* (C-170/78), the UK had a tax on light wines which was roughly five times the tax on beer. The UK produced a lot of beer, but very little wine. The Court of Justice found that light wines were in competition with beer and the UK had breached art.110(2).

Interaction between Article 110(1) and 110(2)

Article 110(1) deals with similar products, whereas art.110(2) aims to prevent unequal tax treatment of goods which are in competition with each other. If a measure breaches art.110(1), the Member State is required to equalise the taxes on domestic and imported products. If a measure breaches art.110(2), the Member State is required to remove the protective effect.

Objective justification

Taxes which indirectly prefer a Member State's traders are capable of being objectively justified. EU law does not prevent the use of tax policy for social objectives provided that the tax was based on an objective criterion, was not discriminatory, and did not have a protective effect.

One example was in *Chemical Farmaceuti v DAF SPA* (C-140/79). There Italy taxed ethyl alcohol fermented from agricultural products at a lower rate than synthetic ethyl alcohol made from a petroleum derivative. This was to promote agriculture and to protect the petroleum for more important uses. These two alcohols could be used interchangeably but Italy did not make much of the synthetic product. The Court held that the implementation of this policy did not lead to any discrimination as it encouraged imports of synthetic ethyl and also hampered Italian production of the petroleum derivative. This was found to be objectively justified and therefore fell out of art.110.

In *Commission v Greece* (C-132/88), Greece had a lower tax rate on cars with smaller engines in order to help combat air pollution. This tax was found to be objectively justified despite the fact that Greece did not produce any cars with larger engines.

The Boundary between Article 110 and Other Articles

Article 30

Both art.110 and art.30 deal with the imposition of financial charges by the state; however, they are mutually exclusive. Article 110 deals with discrimination against goods once they have entered a particular Member State. Article 30 deal with duties or charges levied as a result of a good crossing a border. If a tax is a customs duty or CEE under art.30, this makes it contrary to the Treaty by its very nature and it must be struck down. Charges which fall under art.110, on the other hand, are only incompatible with the Treaty where they are discriminatory or protective.

Denkavit Loire Sarl v France (C-132/78) provides guidance for determining whether art.30 or art.110 applies. France imposed charges on the slaughter of animals in an abattoir and on imported products to ensure a similar taxation system. The Court had to decide whether a French charge on lard was a customs duty or internal taxation. This was held to be a CEE. The Court held:

> "As the court has acknowledged several times, and in particular in [case 46/76 *Bauhuis v the Netherlands*] any pecuniary charge, whatever its designation and mode of application, which is imposed unilaterally on goods by reason of the fact that they cross a frontier and which is not a customs duty in the strict sense, constitutes a CEE ... such a charge however escapes that classification if it constitutes the consideration for a benefit provided in fact for the importer or exporter representing an amount proportionate to the said benefit. It also escapes that classification if it relates to a general system of internal dues supplied systematically and in accordance with the same criteria to domestic products and imported products alike, in which case it does not come within the scope of [art.30] but within that of Article[110] of theTreaty.
>
> It is however appropriate to emphasize that in order to relate to a general system of internal dues, the charge to which an imported

product is subject must impose the same duty on national products and identical imported products at the same marketing stage and that the chargeable event giving rise to the duty must also be identical in the case of both products. It is therefore not sufficient that the objective of the charge imposed on imported products is to compensate for a charge imposed on similar domestic products—or which has been imposed on those products or a product from which they are derived—at a production or marketing stage prior to that at which the imported products are taxed. To exempt a charge levied at the frontier from the classification of a CEE when it is not imposed on similar national products or is imposed on them at different marketing stages or, again, on the basis of a different chargeable event giving rise to duty, because that charge aims to compensate for a domestic fiscal charge applying to the same products—apart from the fact that this would not take into account fiscal charges which had been imposed on imported products in the originating Member State—would make the prohibition on CEEs empty and meaningless.

It is therefore necessary to reply to the first question that a charge which is imposed on meat, whether or not prepared, when it is imported, and in particular on consignments of lard, even though no charge is imposed on similar domestic products, or a charge is imposed on them according to different criteria, in particular by reason of a different chargeable event giving rise to the duty, constitutes a CEE."

ARTICLE 34

Article 34 TFEU deals with quantitative restrictions, the next topic in this chapter. A case will either come under art.110 or art.34: it cannot come under both headings. This was the case in *Kawala* (C-134/07), where the Court decided that a registration fee for imported second-hand vehicles was of a fiscal nature and therefore fell under art.110. This meant that art.34 was not applicable.

QUANTITATIVE RESTRICTIONS

Customs duties and internal taxes are not the only trade measures which Member States can try and impose on goods imported. Quantitative restrictions and measures having an equivalent effect to quantitative restrictions are also forbidden by EU law. Quantitative restrictions were defined in *Geddo* (C-2/73) as "measures which amount to a total or partial restraint on imports or goods in transit". In *Commission v France* (C-232/78) (import of lamb) and *Commission v UK* (C-231/78) (import of potatoes), the CJEU held that the most obvious examples of quantitative restrictions are complete bans or quotas restricting the import or export of a given product by amount or by value. In *R. v Henn and Darby* (C-34/79), UK legislation restricting the importation of pornography from Denmark was considered to be a quantitative restriction. Articles 34–36 TFEU prohibit quantitative restrictions:

> "Article 34
> Quantitative restrictions on imports and all measures having equivalent effect shall be prohibited between Member States.
>
> Article 35
> Quantitative restrictions on exports, and all measures having equivalent effect, shall be prohibited between Member States.
>
> Article 36
> The provisions of Articles 34 and 35 shall not preclude prohibitions or restrictions on imports, exports or goods in transit justified on grounds of public morality, public policy or public security; the protection of health and life of humans, animals or plants; the protection of national treasures possessing Artistic, historic or archaeological value; or the protection of industrial and commercial property. Such prohibitions or restrictions shall not, however, constitute a means of arbitrary discrimination or a disguised restriction on trade between Member States."

Measures Having Equivalent Effect

Not only are quantitative restrictions forbidden, but measures having equivalent effect to a quantitative restriction ("MEQR") are also forbidden. This is similar to the difference between customs duties and CEEs.

It may be difficult in practice to distinguish between a quantitative restriction and a MEQR; however, they are both forbidden. The definition of MEQR has developed through the case law and is less clear than the meaning of quantitative restrictions. At first, the court tried to have a very broad definition of MEQR but more recently has started to take a more restrictive approach.

The first case on MEQR is *Procureur du Roi v Dassonville* (C-8/74). Mr Dassonville was a Belgian trader who bought a consignment of scotch in France and imported it into Belgium. Scotch was much cheaper in France at the time than it was in Belgium as French dealers were selling it cheaply to create a new market of whisky drinkers. Belgian law required a certificate of origin in order to be sold as the UK and Scotland were not part of the customs union at the time. He did not have a certificate as French law did not require one and was prosecuted when he imported this scotch into Belgium. Here the Court held:

> "All trading rules enacted by Member States which are capable of hindering directly or indirectly, actually or potentially, intra-Community trade are to be considered as measures of equivalent effect to quantitative restrictions."

This is a very broad definition. It seems from this that a measure does not have to be discriminatory in order to be caught by art.34. The Dassonville case was followed by *Rewe-Zentral AG v Bundesmonopolverwaltung für Branntwein* (C-120/78) (Cassis de Dijon). Here one of Germany's biggest drinks retailers complained that the German authorities were making it difficult to import and sell Cassis de Dijon. Cassis de Dijon is a French blackberry liqueur. Traditionally it is mixed with white wine and it is around 15 per cent strength. It is the favourite drink of the fictional detective Hercule Poirot. At the time, in order to be called a fruit liqueur in German law, a drink must be at least 25 per cent strength. This meant Cassis de Dijon was legal for sale in France, but not in Germany. This German government policy had effectively banned Cassis de Dijon from the German market and the liqueur could not compete with stronger German liqueurs. The CJEU found that even though the German rules on alcohol levels applied to all drinks from any country, its application to imported products imposed a double burden on foreign drinks and was an MEQR. The Court held:

> "The concept of measures having an effect equivalent to quantitative restrictions on imports ... is to be understood to mean that the fixing of a minimum alcohol content for alcoholic beverages intended for human consumption by the legislation of a Member State also falls within the prohibition laid down in that provision where the importation of alcoholic beverages lawfully produced and marketed in another Member State is concerned."

This affirms the previous statements in *Dassonville*. It can be seen from this that the CJEU wants to support the mutual recognition of goods from different EU Member States. This means that Member States must recognise goods lawfully produced in another Member State and allow them to be sold. The Court added to the *Dassonville* test by saying that MEQR also included so-called indistinctly applicable measures if they could not be explained by mandatory requirements. Indistinctly applicable measures are measures which apply both to domestic and to imported goods.

Indistinctly Applicable Rules

Indistinctly applicable dual burdens are prohibited by art.34 unless they can be justified by one of the mandatory requirements. This is because imported goods are required to comply with two sets of rules: the ones from the Member State where they are made and the ones from the Member State to which they are imported. A good example of a dual burden case is *Walter Rau* (261/81). There Belgium had a law requiring margarine to be sold in cubes so that it would not be confused with butter. This applied both to Belgian and imported margarine. This was held to be an indistinctly applicable dual burden and was struck down. It would be more difficult for non-Belgian producers to comply with this law without incurring extra costs. The Court felt that consumers could be protected just as effectively by other measures, which are less of a restriction on the free movement of goods, for example, labelling rules.

In *Cinéthèque SA v Fédération nationale des cinémas français* (C-60/84), France banned the sale or hire of videos of films during the first year in which the film was shown in cinemas. This law applied equally to domestic and imported videos; its aim was to encourage people to go to the cinema and to promote the making of films. The video-cassette distributors challenged the law. The CJEU held that the law was caught by art.34 but could be justified since it encouraged the creation of films regardless of where they came from.

In *Torfaen BC v B&Q* (C-145/88), the hardware shop B&Q was prosecuted for breaching Sunday trading rules by opening on Sundays. These Sunday trading rules applied to imported and domestic products equally. The Court held that this might be permitted if there was objective justification and the rule was proportionate. It also held that it is up to the national court to decide this.

Keck and Mithouard

The next major case is *Criminal Proceedings against Keck and Mithouard* (C-267–268/91). This case limited the definition of MEQR after it had been extended in the two previous cases. Keck & Mithouard had sold French beer and coffee at a lower price than they had paid for it. At the time, French law prohibited resale at a loss and they were prosecuted. They took a case saying the French law was incompatible with EU law. The Court decided it was necessary to re-examine and clarify its case law on this matter as traders had an increasing tendency to invoke art.34 TFEU to challenge any rules which limited their commercial freedom even where such rules are not aimed at products from other Member States.

The Court found that only rules relating to product requirements such as size, shape, colour, etc should be illegal, while rules relating to selling arrangements such as locations, opening hours, staff requirements, etc will mostly avoid art.34. This was to limit cases to situations where, in the absence of discrimination, there is a real risk of an importer being subject to a dual burden.

SELLING ARRANGEMENTS

Selling arrangements are rules relating to the circumstances in which goods can be sold. Since *Keck*, selling arrangements are equal burden rules which fall outside of the scope of art.34 TFEU. Selling arrangements are measures dealing with where, when, how, and by whom goods may be sold. Rules the Court has found to be selling arrangements include: rules relating to price controls (*Belgapom* (C-63/94)), time of the sale (*Boermans* (C-401–402/92)), and the place of the sale and restrictions on who can sell goods (*Commission v Greece* (C-391/92)).

Advertising rules have also been treated as selling arrangements since *Keck*. *De Agostini* (C-34–36/95) was about a Swedish ban on TV advertising to children under 12. De Agostini is a magazine company specialising in monthly magazines that build up a collection. Here the children's magazine *Everything about Dinosaurs!* from the UK was advertised on Swedish television channels. This magazine series contained information about dinosaurs, as well as parts which built up a glow-in-the-dark dinosaur skeleton. The Court found "television advertising was the only effective form of promotion enabling De Agostini to penetrate the Swedish market," and decided that if a ban affected foreign traders more than domestic ones then it would breach art.34. This means selling arrangements which discriminate against foreign traders may be a MEQR. It is for the national courts to decide on the facts.

In *Gourmet International Products* (C-405/98), Sweden prevented the advertisement of alcohol on the radio, on TV and in magazines. Here the ban was found to affect foreign traders more than domestic ones and was therefore discriminatory. The Court of Justice held the law infringed art.34 but it could be justified on public health grounds if it was proportionate.

Italian Trailers

Commission v Italy (C-11/05) (Italian Trailers) appears to limit *Keck*. There, Italian Highway Code prohibited motorcycles from pulling trailers. No Italian manufacturers made these trailers, they were only made by foreign manufacturers. The Court found that no consumers would buy these products if they could not use them and this would hinder access to the market. The Court gave three situations where a measure would be an MEQR:

1. Where the object/effect of the measure is to treat products from other Member States less favourably than domestic products;
2. When a measure requires goods lawfully made in another Member State to meet another condition even if it applies to all products indiscriminately;
3. Any other measure which hinders the access of products originating in other Member States to the market.

The third situation arose here but the Court found that this could be justified on the grounds of road safety. This approach was confirmed in *Mickelsson* (C-142/05). There the Court of Justice did not refer to *Keck* but used the definition of an MEQR provided in the *Italian Trailers* case. It found the measure would hinder access to the market as it would deter consumers from buying jet-skis but it could be justified on the grounds of the protection of health and life of plants and animals as well as environmental protection.

Situation Now

Quantitative restrictions started in *Dassonville* as:

> "All trading rules enacted by Member States which are capable of hindering directly or indirectly, actually or potentially, intra-Community trade are to be considered as measures of equivalent effect to quantitative restrictions."

In *Cassis de Dijon*, the Court added that quantitative restrictions also included indistinctly applicable measures. In *Keck and Mithouard*, selling arrangements were found to fall outside of art.34 and are therefore not MEQR. In the Italian *Trailers* case, measures hindering market access would be MEQR but it could be justified on the facts. Therefore, art.34 TFEU will apply not only to national measures which discriminate against imported goods, but also to those which, in law, seem to apply equally to both domestic and imported goods, but in practice are more difficult for imports and those which hinder access to the market but will not apply to selling arrangements.

Discriminatory Quantitative Restrictions

Administrative practices

Administrative practices, as well as laws, can be MEQR. It was held in *Commission v Germany* (C-387/99) that an administrative practice can be an MEQR if it is consistent and general. There Germany was in breach of the Treaty for labelling vitamin food supplements from other states as medicines. In *Commission v France* (C-42/82), the Court held that it was an MEQR where France consistently detained large amounts of imported Italian wine for long periods where there were only minor problems with their paperwork. In *Commission v France* (C-21/84) (the franking machine case), French Postal administrations practices amounted to an MEQR where the French authorities consistently refused to approve postal franking machines from other Member States.

Practices of state-supported bodies

In *Commission v Ireland* (C-249/81) (the Buy Irish campaign), the Irish government used the Irish Goods Council to attempt to stimulate the economy by getting Irish people to buy Irish goods. There was an advertising campaign encouraging Irish people to buy Irish Goods instead of foreign ones, a service to tell people where they could buy Irish goods, exhibitions of Irish goods and the Guaranteed Irish symbol was used to promote Irish products. The Irish Goods Council was a private company but was made up of Government appointees, and was financed by the State. The Court of Justice said that it was clearly carrying out Government policy and that the activities had the potential to affect imports from other Member States, and that potential effect was comparable to the effect that might result from any binding measure taken by the Government. The Court also held that it was not relevant that the measures to get Irish companies to put the Guaranteed Irish symbol on their goods were not binding, as they were capable of influencing consumers and were, therefore, a MEQR. Buy Irish and the Guaranteed Irish symbol still continue as they are no longer state-aided: they are now financed privately by Irish goods producers.

Buy Irish can be contrasted with *Apple & Pear Development Council v KJ Lewis* (C-222/82). The Apple and Pear Development Council was a body which promoted British fruit. It was established by the English Government and its members were also appointed by the State. It was financed by fruit growers by order of the State; they had to register with this Council and pay a compulsory annual charge to it. It ran a campaign promoting British Apples and Pears. The Court held that this campaign was not an MEQR as it promoted British fruit but did not advise consumers to give British products preference over foreign fruit.

Origin markings

Origin marking requirements have been found to be quantitative restrictions. These are a requirement that goods come with a marking which shows the country from which they came. In *Commission v Ireland* (C-113/80) (the Irish Souvenirs case), Irish law required imported souvenirs and jewellery to have an origin mark or be labelled as being foreign. The Court held that Member States can only require origin markings where the origin denotes a certain specific characteristic quality in the goods unique to where they come from, such as the requirement that Champagne can only come from the Champagne region in France. Otherwise, origin marking requirements are quantitative restrictions as they make it harder for goods to enter a market. In *Commission v the UK* (C-207/83), a similar English law was struck down as it would increase production costs for imported products and would allow UK consumers to assert any prejudice they had in favour of domestic products.

State inaction

Failure to act by a Member State might result in difficulties for goods entering the state. In *Commission v France* (C-265/95) (Angry Farmers case), the French government failed to take steps to prevent commando groups of angry farmers destroying Spanish strawberries when they crossed the border. The French government was found to be liable under art.34 for this failure to act.

After this case, the Council of the European Union issued Regulation No. 2679/98 (the Strawberry Regulation) which gave the Commission power to intervene in these cases and take the Member State before the CJEU. In order to use this power, there must be the serious disruption of the free movement of goods, serious loss to individuals affected and the necessity of immediate state action.

Justifying Quantitative Restrictions

Under certain circumstances, quantitative restrictions can be justified under art.36 TFEU. This is why certain goods, such as cannabis, can be sold in some Member States, but not in others. We have already seen in *Mickelsson* that a ban on the use of jet skis outside of "general navigable waterways" could be justified on the grounds of protection of health and life of humans, animals or plants. Article 36 lists six exceptions:

- public morality;
- public policy;
- public security;
- protection of health and life of humans, animals or plants;
- protection of national treasures;
- protection of industrial and commercial property.

This is an exhaustive list. *Commission v Italy* (C-95/81) placed a strict interpretation on these exceptions. The courts interpret these exceptions very narrowly and certain conditions that must be met in order to rely on them.

The reason for the exception must be genuine. In *Commission v UK* (C-40/82) (Poultry Imports), the British government restricted the importation of turkeys from other Member States just before Christmas. They claimed this was on public health grounds to prevent the spread of Newcastle disease. The Court found this was really to block imports of French turkeys rather than to protect health.

National measures must be proportionate. The Court in *Commission v Italy* (C-128/89) held:

> "National rules adopted in order to achieve one of the objectives referred to in Article 36 [TFEU] are compatible with the Treaty only in so far as they do not exceed the limits of what is appropriate and necessary in order to achieve the desired objective."

In *Scottish Whiskey Association v The Advocate General for Scotland* (C-333/14), a recent case on the lawfulness of a Scottish measure to introduce minimum alcohol pricing (MPU), the Court noted in relation to proportionality

> "that burden of proof cannot extend to creating the requirement that, where the competent national authorities adopt national legislation imposing a measure such as the MPU, they must prove, positively, that no other conceivable measure could enable the legitimate objective pursued to be attained under the same conditions."

Public morality

In *R. v Henn and Darby*, UK law restricting the importation of pornography from Denmark was a quantitative restriction; however, the Court of Justice held that it could be justified under the grounds of public policy and public morality. This was despite the fact that UK law did not prohibit the possession of pornography. Both the films and the magazines depicted explicit sexual activities which were illegal in the UK. The films included scenes of violence and two of the magazines contained only photographs of naked girls between about five and fourteen years old engaging in sexual activity with an adult man. Five of the magazines contained advertisements inviting readers to apply to a "Model Contact". This quantitative restriction was justified.

In *Conegate v Commisioners for Customs and Exercise* (C-121/85), Conegate imported life-size inflatable dolls from Germany to the UK. They claimed that, because of the dolls' realistic physical features, they were for use as models for the window displays of ladies' dresses and underwear. The customs officials inspected the consignments and found that they contained a number of inflatable life size rubber dolls described as "Love Love Dolls", "Miss World Specials" and "Rubber Ladies", and there were also a number of "Sexy Vacuum Flasks". The Court held that EU law allows each state to make their own assessment on whether something is indecent or obscene; however, the fact that goods cause offence cannot be regarded as sufficiently serious to justify restrictions on the free movement of goods where the Member State does not adopt criminal laws against making, marketing or distributing such goods in its territory.

Public policy

The public policy grounds has been very narrowly interpreted by the Court of Justice. In *R. v Bouchereau* (C-30/77), it held that reliance on that exception presupposed the existence of "a genuine and sufficiently serious threat to the requirements of public policy that affects one of the fundamental interests of society". There is only one example where this has been successfully invoked. In *R. v Thompson* (C-7/78), the British government banned the exportation of gold coins by a collector in order to protect the Royal Mint. There it was held that:

> "A ban on exporting such coins with a view to preventing their being melted down or destroyed in another Member State is justified on grounds of public policy within the meaning of Article 30 Treaty, because it stems from the need to protect the right to mint coinage which is traditionally regarded as involving the fundamental interests of the State."

Public security

In *Campus Oil* (C-72/83), the Irish government requested that companies use 35 per cent oil from a state-owned refinery on grounds of public security. The Court of Justice found this to be an acceptable defence as oil is such an important energy source and interruptions to its supply could affect public security. However, in recent years, the Court has clarified that the Campus Oil case should be considered an exception to a rule, not a leading authority. It was held in *Commission v Greece* (C-398/98) that the reason for this is that other energy sources are not as important to running a country as oil is.

In *Richardt* (C-367/89), computer chips which were being exported to Moscow, then capital of the Soviet Union, were seized by the authorities in Luxembourg on public security grounds when the transporter did not have a license to transport strategically sensitive goods. It was held that state security includes internal and external security, although seizing goods may be disproportionate when they could be returned to their state of origin instead.

Protection of health, animals and plants

This is the most frequently used defence to quantitative restrictions. Protection of health is a fundamental interest of all Member States. According to several cases, the protection of health, animals and plants comes before other public interests. When considering this defence, the Court of Justice will examine whether there is a real health risk, as in the Christmas turkeys case, and whether there is a seriously considered health policy. In *Rewe-Zentralfinanz* (C-4/75), Germany had rules requiring inspection of imported apples to control spread of the San Jose Bug. It was held that there was a real risk of the pest spreading and that whilst the inspection was a MEQR, it was justified because inspection was needed to protect domestic apples.

In *Commission v Italy* (C-420/01), Italy prohibited the marketing of energy drinks containing caffeine in excess of certain limits, claiming that high levels of caffeine may harm health. However, the Italian authorities did not show that the restriction was necessary and proportionate. The scientific evidence that Italy based their claims on did not consider that this prohibition was valid. In fact, the latest research had proven that energy drinks containing high doses of caffeine did not show any risk to health. The Court held that "by applying to drinks produced and marketed in other Member States a rule prohibiting the marketing in Italy of energy drinks containing caffeine in excess of a certain limit, without showing that that limit is necessary and proportionate for the protection of public health", Italy had failed to fulfil its obligations under art.34.

Sandoz (C-174/82) deals with the situation where the scientific evidence is uncertain as to risks to human health etc. There, a Dutch rule prohibited the sale of muesli bars with added vitamins. At the time, scientific consensus was unclear as to whether consuming too many vitamins was a health risk. It was held that:

> "insofar as there are uncertainties at the present state of scientific research it is for the Member States, in the absence of harmonization, to decide what degree of protection of the health and life of humans they intend to assure, having regard however for the requirements of the free movements of goods."

Commission v Denmark (C-192/01) confirms this. Member States must examine the scientific evidence and if is still uncertain, Member States can rely on the precautionary principle. They do not have to wait for conclusive scientific evidence before addressing a potential risk to health etc.

Protection of national treasures possessing artistic, historic or archaeological value

This exception clearly draws from the Italian Art Treasures case. There is no case law in this area because of two pieces of legislation: Regulation 3911/92 and Directive 93/7.

Protection of industrial and commercial property

This exception covers trademarks, copyright, patents and other similar rights. The Court in *Keurkoop v Nancy Kean Gifts* (C-144/81) held that the protection of designs came under this exception. In *Allen and Handburys Ltd v Generics (UK) Ltd* (C-434/85), there was an attempt to stop the importation of a good which infringed a patent. There it was held that this exception cannot constitute a means of arbitrary discrimination or a disguised restriction of trade between Member States. The Court found an injunction against the importer would constitute arbitrary discrimination and was not justified on the grounds of this exception. The Irish government attempted to rely on this defence in the *Irish Souvenirs* case but was unsuccessful. In *Commission v France (Parts in Transit)* (C-23/99), the Court found that detaining suspected counterfeit goods for ten days was disproportionate to the purpose of an inspection and could not be justified under this ground. One case where this was successfully invoked was *Hoffman la Roche v Centrafarm* (C-102/77) where it was held that the right to prevent a trademark being reapplied to repackaged goods was justified on this ground.

Index